ESCAPE FROM THE
TWISTED
PLANET

ESCAPE FROM THE TWISTED PLANET

HAROLD L. MYRA

WORD BOOKS
PUBLISHER
WACO, TEXAS

A DIVISION OF
WORD, INCORPORATED

ESCAPE FROM THE TWISTED PLANET
By H.L. Myra

Formerly published under the title, NO MAN IN EDEN

ISBN 0-8499-2949-0
Library of Congress Catalog Number: 68-56989
PRINTED IN THE UNITED STATES OF AMERICA

Scripture quotations used in this book are from *Living Psalms and Proverbs,* Paraphrased by Kenneth N. Taylor, copyright 1967 by Tyndale House, Publishers. Used by permission.

The author acknowledges his debt to many writers and speakers, among them C.S. Lewis, J.R.R. Tolkien, Ray Bradbury, Malcolm Cronk, and Jay Kesler....

To my mother, who happily put up with
the birth pangs of my writing,
and to my wife Jeanette who responded
to incessant new ideas and 3 A.M.
"brainstorming," and added a woman's
insight into plotting, characterization, dialogue.

A WORD FROM THE AUTHOR

Although only a dozen years have passed since this book first appeared, eons have flickered by in fantasy/science fiction. *Star Wars* and its imitators have filled both screens and store displays. Books of this genre have gone from moderate sales to extensive industries. Our interest in other worlds has grown enormously.

Escape from the Twisted Planet, originally titled *No Man in Eden,* was written in the youth-dominated sixties, and rereading it is like a time-warp into both past and future. This embryonic first novel causes me ambivalence because its rough edges could use some brisk sanding; yet its readers seem oblivious to that. Whenever someone comes up to me and says with great intensity, "I love your book," they always mean this one. People write or call, chagrined that it's been out of print, wanting to secure any sort of copy.

So I welcome this edition as well as those readers who will relax with it and let their minds flow with the ideas, for its appeal is in its flight of imagination.

Every one of us will be in another world before long, and we will be thinking, feeling, communicating. . . . Perhaps that is why we find imaginings about God's full creation—hinted at throughout the Bible from Genesis and Ezekiel and Daniel through John and Revelation—so intriguing and challenging. We know that we muse about not only speculations of fantastic worlds, but eternal realities which, though seen through a glass darkly now, will be very clear to each of us in those next worlds.

HAROLD L. MYRA

Look up into the heavens! Who created all these stars? As a shepherd leads his sheep, calling each by its pet name, and counts them to see that none are lost or strayed, so God does with stars and planets.

Isaiah 40:26
Living Psalms and Proverbs

1

David Koehler stabbed at his typewriter keys, then stared at the line he had just written. His news release about The Union Jacks simply would not jell.

His eyes wandered slowly around his small den. The events of last night were soaked into every part of him, like some oppressing, heavy liquid. It was part of him; his emotions could not be freed, whether he turned up the stereo so it physically shook the room or went out to the kitchen and laughed and joked with Charlotte. It had been too bizarre to be real; it had been too real to have been fantasy.

David watched as the antelope skin on the floor slowly rose in the center, took form and grew a head with black, pointed antlers. It kicked at his typewriter, then ran off through the wall, out of which emerged a little, laughing Indian fakir in thick red-and-green-plaid flowing robes. The fakir sat on the floor while the tomahawk from the wall floated toward him and suddenly swished through the air at the little man's head. The fakir instantly shrank, disappearing through a tiny crack in the floor as the tomahawk kept swinging and finally swished over to hook its wall mate—the Indian headdress—and dropped it on the crack.

The walls started shifting in a circular pattern to the left, the antelope returned, and one by one The Union Jacks were crawling and then leaping out of the typewriter, growing to massive proportions and drowning out the stereo with their own gigantic beat and obscene gestures.

A wry expression grew on David's face. Almost any other time he could let his imagination go like this, and it gave him amused relaxation. He especially wanted his little game to somehow put last night's events into perspective—that is, into a class of fantasy that could be dispelled as easily as his musing thoughts.

But the oppressive heaviness still seeped through him. Something *had* happened last night, and it was as tangible as the typewriter keys under his fingers. The memory of those flashing lights, weird things . . . he wanted it to be a dream, yet he knew it hadn't been.

It was 9:30 P.M. David wanted to whip through these releases and be done with them—he resented his having had to bring work home. As he rose to put on another record, he noticed Charlotte peeking through the louvered doors, smiling, a tray in her hands.

"Safe to enter the bear's den?" she asked. He smiled back at her: he always made it a point to emphasize that the den was for work, and she kidded him about his bear's growl.

"Sustenance for the laborer," she said, bringing the food in and placing it on his coffee table—an old $5 trunk he had painted cherry red with black handles and metal corners.

"You know what I like about you?" Charlotte asked, sitting on the arm of his easy chair.

He shook his head and took a bite of cake roll.

"You're conscientious . . . and intelligent . . . and friendly . . . and sensitive . . . and cute . . . and . . ." she paused dramatically, then burrowed her nose into his cheek ". . . and snuggly."

He kissed her—lightly, then with just a little force—and settled her on the side of his chair as they ate. He could tell she was still concerned about what had happened to him last night, even though she was trying to hide it. Being a psych major, she couldn't just drop it from her mind.

"Do you realize, young lady," David asked with mock severity, "that Thursday is our two-month anniversary? And

(14)

do you realize that we haven't so much as glanced at our wedding book in weeks? Now that's sheer neglect, and I suggest we prepare for this auspicious anniversary by getting nostalgic right now—with the pictures."

Charlotte gave him a big grin and wink, bounced off to get the photos, and returned with not only the album but a packet of clippings. For the next half hour they talked and laughed about rice which had stayed in their clothes for hours, the late usher, the bridesmaid who made a flying leap and caught the bridal bouquet. There was one picture David especially liked of Charlotte—she was tossing the bouquet, a delightful, candid smile on her face, her graceful figure in lithe motion.

He pulled the photo out of the book and studied it closely. He knew it was not just his lover's eyes which saw an entrancing smile and striking soft-blonde hair and delicate features. She had been a beautiful, beautiful bride.

He stared overlong at it, letting a smile play at the corners of his mouth, then from deep in his throat let out an appreciative "Gggggrrrufff!!!!!"

She kissed him perkily on the forehead. "Thank you!"

"And then, there's me," he lamented, picking up a shot showing him and his best man horsing around with the carnations before the ceremony. David was a nice looking guy—but it was obvious Charlotte was cuter.

"Ah well," he intoned with mock dramatics, "at least I am uh . . . er . . . uh . . . snuggly."

She laughed, grabbed him by the hair and kissed him again.

"Now," David asked, "aren't you glad you didn't marry old Steve Forsyth! He would definitely *not* have been the snuggly type."

"Well," she said teasingly, twisting her lips, "you just never know about that sort of thing. Besides—he isn't *old*—no more than twenty-three!"

"Oh, I didn't mean ancient—just 'good old Steve Forsyth.' You know, the typical, handsome, after-you-for-years, young-man-on-the-way-up Steve Forsyth. *Nothing* compared to me. I'm intelligent and conscientious and . . ."

"And I love you," she interrupted. "And I'm going to make sure you stay all those things by sticking around and keeping you humble and snuggly for the next eighty years!"

She started gathering up the dishes. "I'm also going to get out of your way so you can get those things done before midnight."

Charlotte kissed him, then whisked out.

He rose, put on the only album he had of The Union Jacks, and with a grimace sat down to finish the copy.

But his fingers dawdled on the keys. The events of the night before swirled around in his mind like dark spectres. He tried to understand it all: his imaginative mind could have conjured up such an episode, and he wanted to believe that was what had happened last night. For though he loved creating strange and different plots, he also had a factual, logical mind.

He had inherited and developed this through his father, a prosperous lawyer—and a skilled logician and freethinker whom he held in great respect. However, his mother, a church woman, had been very concerned that he find some sort of faith.

As David fingered the typewriter keys, he thought back to the conversations he used to have with his mother. He had always loved debate. Through high school and college, he enjoyed the challenge of competition. He could remember his basic points and maneuver an opponent. And when it came to his mother, he had infinitely more facts at his disposal than did she. One of their conversations seemed especially apropos to the eerie events of the night before.

"Mother, have you ever really studied the Inquisition?" he had asked her on a Thanksgiving vacation from college. "For the sake of religion, they would stretch people on this rack, see, and pull them to the breaking point, then tap their joints, and they'd fall apart. Or they'd brand them. Or cook them alive. Then there were thumbscrews and foot twisters and all the other godly devices to make bad people turn good."

"But they were Catholics," she protested.

"Aha! Mother, let me give you all the details on the exquisitely painful executions the Protestants prepared for the Catholics!"

"Oh, they just didn't understand things in those days."

"I thought Martin Luther was a hero," David would retort. "He cheered people on when they murdered Anabaptists. And how about the Crusades, Mom? They sure butchered a lot of pagans in the name of Christ, who said to 'love your neighbor.' Have you ever read what Christians did on our continent—besides burning 'witches'?" He picked up a book he'd brought specially for this. "Clement Wood in *A History of the World* says that the Spaniards killed every Indian in Cuba. They'd burn them at the stake. The governor of Yucatan would grab Indian kids and feed them to his dogs. In San Domingo, they'd wrap them in straw and roast 'em over a slow fire. When Spaniards went on trips, they'd take live Indians along for dog food. Nice guys, huh? More than 600,000 died as beasts of burden in Nicaragua. The population of Jamaica and Puerto Rico went from 600,000 to—*would you believe*—200! A total of *twenty million* Indians were killed!"

His mother glared at him with a disgusted look, tossing it off with, "Oh, go on! Those were soldiers doing that, not real Christians."

"Oh, that's *just* the point," David charged back. "Wood says these Spaniards were sure they were on a sacred mission. These Indians were pagans, and they had to convert them."

David could slice up her arguments, tearing down all reports of the supernatural as myth exploited by power structures to maintain control over people. "Sure—religion can have a place," he would tell his mother. "You can build something up in your mind that has high ideals and meaning. But society without religion isn't chaos. Look at Russia. Economically they've come a long way. No, they're not perfect—but their individual moral standards are higher than ours! If religion is so vital, why haven't they fallen apart over there?"

Perhaps this pattern of thinking is why David was so loath to accept the events of the night before.

* * *

He had been driving home from his office. As he topped a rise, he saw a bluish light out in a field about a quarter mile away—and almost at the same time, his motor died.

He kept staring at the light, which became a diffused red, orange, and green, and vainly tried to restart his engine. Finally, he got out, pushed the car to the shoulder, and left it there, keeping his eyes on the light before him. Curious, exhil-

(17)

arated, he hesitated, then crouched and started to walk along the highway toward it. There had been a number of reported UFO incidents in David's Pennsylvania community of Bellwood, but he had quickly discounted them as misinterpretations of natural phenomena or psychological aberrations.

He was getting close and the light increased in intensity and color. David edged away from the road into an unplowed field of weeds to avoid detection, and as he continued moving toward the object, speculations about its origin churned in his brain.

Finally, he was almost upon it. There was no question now —it looked like some kind of huge jet, but it wasn't a conventional craft. The metal glowed from the pulsating, bright lights around the entire ship. It was a perfectly round disc, like two saucers, one inverted on top of the other, with the two rims forming large portholes about five feet square. The entire craft was the size of his school gym. It rested under a tall bank where shale had been clawed from the earth by shovels.

As David approached the craft, he almost crawled as he circled to the higher ground above it. The obvious solidity and reality of the strange, brilliantly lighted spectacle made him think first of experimental craft, whether Russian or American. Something this obviously real had to have a tangible explanation.

Now he was so close along the edges of the shale pit that he could have thrown a rock at one of the portholes and easily hit it. He could see something like rooms behind the transparent substance which made up the windows; equipment and possibly furniture of some kind made up shadowy silhouettes inside.

Now David pulled himself closer on his belly, right out to the lip of the cliff directly over the craft. He glanced toward the city. The colored brightness must have been lighting up the black horizon for miles. Surely others were seeing this. Surely they would be here soon. There had to be some way to capture this thing or to find out what it was all about.

But then again, if it were an advanced military craft of some kind, how could he do anything more than just lie here and observe until it lifted off?

How would the craft do that, though? There were no wings,

no rotor blades, nothing to give it flight. It was like a huge, flattened egg nestled beside the bank of the shale pit. It did not resemble an aircraft at all, except possibly as a free-floating object from an astronaut's space ship.

Pulling himself closer, out over the lip of the shale, David wondered if he could somehow lower himself to look directly into one of the portholes. Then, as he put his weight on the outer edge, a small portion of shale under his hand gave way. It was just enough to throw him off balance and start him sliding downward. David twisted his body backwards to regain the top, but he couldn't.

In terror he realized he was falling right on top of the craft. Even as he fell, thoughts of scrambling off and dropping to the ground pounded in his brain. But he never had the chance. The craft's reaction to his body's hitting the solid metal was almost instantaneous. It started a direct ascent, and before David could regain his senses, he was grasping on to a metal ridge and looking down to a drop of thirty feet.

The craft kept rising higher and higher, until he could look down on the trees and houses below as if from a Piper Cub lazily circling. His balance was precarious. The metal was perfectly smooth, like some kind of reddish-bronze steel, except for a thick ridge along the outer edge. He spread-eagled himself with his fingers clutching the lifesaving ridge and his feet stretching back toward the craft's center to give him stability.

But there was no stability, for the motion accelerated toward the east and the wind started tearing at his handholds, almost lifting his body.

The speed increased more and more, and he felt the tearing wind nearly rip him from the craft . . . and he began to scream in a terror he'd never even come close to experiencing before, a terror like that of a man plummeting from a high building with no hope of rescue.

2

As if in answer to his screams, the ship slowed down. It hovered for perhaps five full, long minutes, and then he saw a metal arm with a blunt, no-fingered "hand" beginning to extend from a small opening about eight feet away. The arm had flexible joints every two feet and began moving toward David as if to encircle and pull him toward itself.

He shrank back, but the arm kept coming closer in a wide, tightening circle. He could not have leaped over it because of the probability of a fall. As it touched him, he grasped the thing and twisted himself over it and outside the circle.

At that moment, the space ship began moving forward, as if to show David its alternatives. As the wind began tearing at him again, the arm bent back the other way with its flexible joints, encircled him, and slowly drew him to a hole in the craft, which opened further and further, like a camera lens. Suddenly, he pulled himself along the arm and down into the orifice, knowing it was the only path to possible safety.

After sliding down the metal arm about ten feet, he found himself in a room shaped like a thin slice of pie, with a porthole making up the outer curved edge. The walls, floor, and ceiling were made of an exotic, burnished metal. It all reminded him of a surgical room. Yet except for the expanse of window, there was nothing of interest to be seen—not even the arm which had pulled him in, nor evidence of the aperture above through which he had come.

He crawled over to the porthole and saw clearly the ground below. He was now traveling at a fast rate of speed, which reminded him very much of jet trips he'd taken from New York to Chicago. The craft was well above a layer of clouds which distorted the lights below. David continued to stare at the earth and clouds as the travel continued for about fifteen minutes. Then they were over the ocean. Their speed increased greatly, and thoughts began to whirl in his brain about Russia and secret bases and extraterrestrial life.

Then the craft slowed to a point of hovering. Suddenly, it floated downward, like a saucer through water, seemingly uncontrolled. His stomach jumped badly, with the feeling of a high roller coaster dip, and he knew that for the first time he might very well become sick and lose his last meal.

The craft hit the water with a gigantic splash and continued sinking at a slower rate. After about five minutes, it apparently settled on the bottom, with nothing visible through the porthole but blackness, and within the little room, a luminous light which came from the metal itself.

It was perhaps a half hour that David lay there, trying to still his stomach and calm the fear that pounded through his chest and mind, and to rationally answer all this. But none of his conjectures gave him satisfaction.

As he contemplated getting up and walking around to investigate his original point of entry, a triple set of arms began extending itself from the opposite wall. One arm was just about the level of his chin, and the others were a little lower, with semi-circular brackets coming toward his two arms, as if to pin him against the wall. He tried to dodge them, but they were quicker than his reflexes, and soon he was trapped against the translucent porthole.

It was then that the fear began to well up like a sucking whirlpool from his stomach and ripple out through his entire body. For he saw that at the end of the arm at chin level was what could best be described as a surgeon's scalpel, made of a reddish, glowing metal, deliberately advancing toward him.

His mind flashed to Poe's "The Pit and the Pendulum," and the horror that man must have felt became David's own. Whether terrestrial or extraterrestrial, Russian scientists or men from another world, David was quickly convinced that he would be dissected the same as he himself would have carelessly dissected a frog in biology class, and that he would never know the truth about this fantastic end of his life.

The scalpel came to his chin, then lowered and moved to the point at his throat just above the top button of his sport shirt. He wrenched against the imprisoning arms and rammed his neck back against the porthole to escape it. But the blade inexorably moved closer, and he was firmly pinioned. It started to move down, curving itself toward the sternum, and David desperately rammed his chin at it to shove it aside.

But the immovable blade began to rip down, tearing through his shirt, past his chest and on down through his trousers. The blade never touched his flesh; it worked so delicately, and soon even his shoes were cut away, and the pile of clothes were pulled back across the floor and into a sliding aperture. David's arms were then released, and the emotional trauma of it was enough to send him crumpling to the floor like a stringless puppet.

Being near death twice in such a short time had drained him of strength, fogged his mind, and created a sickness throughout his body which could be cured by nothing but sweet dirt or living room floor beneath him. But nothing of the sort came, and he lay there for another forty minutes or so, trying to regain his capabilities.

Finally, David noticed a movement at the far wall. Entire sections started sliding back, and before long he was in a room at least ten times as large as the smaller one in which he had been confined. It, too, was shaped like a slice of pie, but one comprising about a fourth of an entire circle. The room was dimly but very pleasantly lighted, with soft blues and greens and a velvety floor. The objects in the room seemed like furniture of some sort. Heavily textured fabrics of various colors—something like exotic tweeds—covered large, flowing forms much like couches. Soft, wood-like elements complemented the fabrics in what looked a little like consoles and tables. Everywhere, brilliantly colored plants were arranged ingeniously to complete the effect.

A movement back in the blue-green shadows caught his eye. Then a figure rose from a long, low rise of sea-green tweed and walked toward him, staring intently in his direction. David felt an immense sense of relief at seeing the person before him. He wore no clothes, but his body was unquestionably human-like. His skin was burnished bronze which caught little snatches of light from the room. He moved with an athlete's grace and towered a muscular seven feet tall. David had the sensation he was looking at another race beyond Negro, Caucasian, and Oriental. This burnished bronze figure was unique, with dynamic grace, piercing azure eyes and squarish face—

a handsome person, deeply mature, as if he were very old in a young, alert body. He gripped David's chin with his fingers and palm, as if in greeting, then smiled and led him to a tall, narrow plateau against a wall where he indicated David should sit.

For what happened next David was totally unprepared. Suddenly, the person was communicating to him, but was using no words. He was almost overwhelmed by the force of the creature's thoughts flowing into his mind. He could tell, too, that at the same time the creature was assimilating every thought that raced through his mind.

He knew that brain waves were real, physical things and that theoretically such communication would be possible, but the enormity of finding himself in the mind of someone else and his own mind invaded by another was frustrating. If this were an experiment with a fellow student, or any ordinary person, it would be endurable. But this powerful mind which was reading his own and flowing thoughts into it was such an active, alive thing, probing, analyzing, learning, and informing so rapidly that it was like having a living computer to cope with, something infinitely beyond his mentality.

The creature sensed this and slowed down his own thoughts, but at the same time apparently picked up every one of the earthling's. David found himself answering most of the questions by reflex thoughts.

"Why did you wear such thick coverings on a warm day?" the earth visitor was asking. David tried to convey two thoughts in response: to look right in his society, which he could tell was quite clear and comprehensible to the creature, and to be clothed, not naked. The latter was not comprehensible. In fact, the clear thought in David's mind intrigued but at the same time mystified him. Obviously, the humanoid felt no more naked than a gazelle.

"And how is it that everything on this planet is ancient?" he was being asked. The full-orbed thought projected into his mind included not only the visitor's reaction to earth as being out of date, but carried also a glimpse into the visitor's own highly advanced civilization. The word ancient denoted in the creature's mind the very beginnings of his own culture.

"You can answer that better than I," David thought, moving

his lips as a first grader does in learning to read silently. "With your sophisticated equipment, surely you listen to our radio and TV and know of our civilization's development."

"No. This is forbidden. We explore anywhere and observe you, but we can never make contact."

"You made contact with me."

"No. You contacted *me*—and I must get instructions on precisely what to do with you."

David again felt fear rising in his throat. And he could tell that the creature sensed it and was again mystified—as if these were alien feelings to him. David surmised that his race must have evolved to such a high social order and have conquered their environments so completely that they had lost all fears and inhibitions.

He certainly could not keep back his own fear, for even if this creature knew nothing of fighting and killing, he had been using a scalpel—of which David had such painful memories—and if an order from his superiors instructed him to eliminate the earthling, he might do it with no compunctions whatever. Yet these fears were the opposite of the emotions he had been feeling since the creature had first appeared, for there was such a pleasantness about him and such a happy touch to the interior that he had felt somewhat at ease—until now, as thoughts of his possible fate began to press in on his brain.

The disconcerting thing was that the creature was reading each thought and was more and more perplexed by them, for such thoughts include specifics, of course, such as being sliced through the throat, or being shot like a torpedo into the sea to be crushed by the pressure at this depth, or to be tossed out 50,000 feet above earth. To these thoughts the creature showed bewilderment.

"Why," David asked, "did you cut away my clothing?"

The thoughts which entered David's mind indicated it had been done on command of some superior force, to guard against the devious use of concealed weapons. "But how is it," the humanoid asked, "that there are no people here except on this small planet? We have seen none other."

Again he thought back, as a reflex action, that his host should surely know the answer to that far better than he, for

David had never been more than a few thousand feet above the ground.

There was an intense curiosity in this brain of immense prowess which was probing his. Yet at the same time that magnificent brain was troubled in some strange way with David's answers and his frame of mind—as if it were coming into contact with something repulsive. David resented that. Yet the creature was so very courteous, and seemingly buoyed up constantly with a full aliveness and joy, that it was difficult not to feel simply like a little mouse in a benign scientist's laboratory, knowing nothing of what was behind the doctor's thinking.

After more talking—or more precisely, thinking—the creature sensed David's exhaustion. He stood, touched something on a wall, and as the wall slid away, he directed him to an inviting little room, with thick layers of soft pastel substances intricately woven, and a plateau about eight feet square which apparently served as a bed, with colored walls and ceiling giving a subdued rainbow effect throughout.

Suddenly he was alone. He paused a moment, then moved to the adjoining bathroom, or so he figured it to be. There were no facilities fashioned of crockery but there was a tiny informal garden with small elevated pools and waterfalls. Returning to the first enclosure, he lay down on the soft but sheetless and blanketless plateau.

When he awoke from his heavy sleep, he noticed his clothes on the higher plateau. On inspection, they were in the same order as they were when he had entered the space craft. How they could have been repaired without stitches was mystifying.

He donned his clothes and went in search of his host, who was in the larger room, seated near one of the translucent portholes. It seemed as if he were fixed in a trance, or more probably talking to someone in the same manner he had talked to David the evening before. But no one was in sight.

The man turned his head and greeted him with a thought which seemed strange. It would have been impossible to put into words, but it was something like, "How absorbed we are in pleasures to meet another morning with the All of All flowing through us." It seemed like a typical "Good morning" greeting from the man.

He led David past another sliding wall into what he hoped was a dining room. It was laid out simply with sections on which to sit and elevated areas beside them. Several murals dominated the decor, depicting both men and women of his race in various activities such as singing, painting, teaching, or designing.

After they sat down, the creature went into his trance or whatever it was for a moment, then looked up, after which he pushed some buttons. As he did, food appeared on the table—a huge variety of shapes and sizes, but none having any familiarity whatever. Apparently, the food had come up through panels in the table top.

The china—actually wide, flat slabs of metal—was exquisitely decorated, but at each plate there was only one utensil. David picked it up and found it to be curiously made—flexible in fact. With a small push on the side it would assume different shapes, which, David assumed, were useful in getting at various types of food.

So it proved. The host started eating with obvious enjoyment at the wide variety before him, and David followed suit.

To say that he enjoyed the meal would be an exaggeration. The taste was so foreign to him that even though he supposed by the elaborate serving that these were marvelous delicacies, he enjoyed the foods only slightly.

His host continued to ask questions and also commented on David's dreams of the evening before. On noting his surprise, the humanoid recounted them and at the telling David pulled out of the fuzziness of his mind his dreams of a few hours before.

Later, the man showed him other parts of the craft. The living room-recreation center was more than anything else a triumph of miniaturization. By what must have been computerized machines and elements far more efficient than silicone wafers, the man could select from millions of songs in one recorder unit. He played several, but the music was beyond David's capability to comprehend. It was exquisite, the voices were full and dynamic, and the variation—ahh, the variation—that was what thrilled David most, for the rich differences of the types of music and the voices and the styles depicted a vast, diverse culture that gloried in originality and creativity, from people who were very distinct personalities.

David thought of his host. He was probably the engineering and adventurer type, glorying in exploration and challenge. Possibly not too musical, not too poetic.

"Yes, you're not far off," his host supplied by thought. It startled David to know that his mind was still being read and that he could conceal nothing from the man.

In the same room were many types of entertainment media, including total 3-D, in which in a play or choreography from a musical composition, in brilliant colors, would introduce the full forms of people, as if they were actually moving about right in the room. The same effect was used with a dramatic story. David was told, too, that in the humanoid's own galaxy he could communicate with his wife at any time in the same way, having her full person, not just an ethereal character, to talk and respond to. Not that she would really be there, but technology made it fully appear so.

The delights of that room were hard to leave. Dramatic stories intrigued but also puzzled him, for though they were widely varied in subject matter and of such excellence that he feared they were beyond his intellect—certainly he caught but little of the frequent touches of humor—the drama never entailed the classic good versus evil. Yet strangely its absence took none of the zest from the productions.

His host also showed him a room full of intricate machinery. Then they walked through other rooms, the purposes of which were not explained, and through several sleeping areas, each beautifully furnished. Returning to the first large room, they sat down and the host explained: "I was given permission to share with you like this, and to allow you to ask questions. Unless I am told not to, I will answer each one."

Of course, questions had been flowing through his mind from the beginning, but his host had kept probing his mind so actively that the thought flow up to this point had been decidedly one way.

"Where is your civilization?" David thought.

"In the same plane as yours. But a very great distance away. How do you measure, that I may be specific?"

"In light years—the speed of light traveling for a year."

"A year?"

David tried to collect his thoughts for a moment, then put them together as, "The amount of time for the earth to travel in its orbit around the sun—365 rotations of the earth on its axis."

The host rose, went into another room, and two minutes later came back with the figures. "According to your measurements, then, my home specifically would be seventeen billion light years away. The end of Zoir—your galaxies—is about ten billion light years from here."

The vastness of that figure made him almost doubt the man, but David's very thought was interrupted by, "Oh, the figures are correct. The machine has innumerable counterchecks against error."

To travel ten billion years at the speed of light! Surely this man hadn't been traveling those blocks of time!

The man was smiling. "No, speeds can greatly excel that of light, in geometric progression, so that it takes relatively little time to travel immense distances."

"But Einstein—uh, one of our scientists," David explained. "He said that the maximum speed attainable was the speed of light. That as a body approaches this speed, time slows, and mass converts to energy."

"Yes, I understand that long ago in our culture it was thought the same. But there are ways of overcoming that."

They communicated for some length then about space and distance, and their flow of thoughts brought him to reports and conjectures David had been reading about. Quasars—brilliant heavenly bodies estimated to be ten billion light years away, the furthest things ever detected and brighter than any star could be. . . . David had read articles linking these with antimatter—the theoretical substance, supposedly the mirror of the matter we know. If brought into contact with matter, antimatter would explode more violently than any nuclear explosion. Some writers theorized that the quasars were gigantic confrontations of matter with antimatter.

The creature had been following his thoughts, and as he became aware of this, David asked, "Has any of this the possibility of truth? Could your world be antimatter?"

"You are indeed close to truth—but *you* are the antimatter."

"Well, of course," David remonstrated. For the first time since his entering of the ship, he felt a trifle superior. "From your point of view, you're matter. But from mine, *you're* the antimatter."

"No, there is a very important distinction," the man quickly disagreed. "*You* and your galaxies are the antimatter. All else is matter. You are part of the great void of the universe, the desolation, out of harmony since the great catastrophe."

He looked at the humanoid sharply. David's mind simply could not keep up—the distances involved staggered his imagination. Ten billion light years! He could conceive of nothing in relation to a billion, and to travel at the speed of light for that distance! Einstein's theories of space and time enfolding back on themselves were so much more comforting than these which the man was pouring into him about space continuing indefinitely, ever greater and greater, until this little ten-billion-light-year expanse became a relatively tiny thing. And beyond the infinity of this plane were *innumerable other dimensions* of space and time equally infinite.

David could not keep up with the complex thoughts of the other and finally, to bring them to more concrete terms, asked, "And who is your ruler?" If he could understand their power structure, possibly he would find the keys to the ultimate questions. He probed for the right thoughts to express ruler, superior.

In the next moments, it was conveyed to David that the man before him was himself the leader of an entire planet, all the people of which had originated from him. He and his wife were patriarch and matriarch. Older than he was a leader of about thirty planets, and above him was a ruler of many hundreds of planets, and above him a patriarch of thousands. All this was based on specific areas of space, not just spheroids, because often gigantic man-made structures extended or free-floated in space. Above these there were the sires of literally millions of planets, and as the space visitor explained, the concepts grew much, much too large for him to convey.

The vastness of the universe had always awed David. But to think of huge populations of living beings out there, inhabiting a universe of far more than empty space and barren planets, made his mind reel.

"Who, then," David asked, "is in charge of everything beyond the quasars?"

"In our plane—our dimension—the first-born creature of our race still lives, and leads all. But as I am led by my telora and each one above me is led by his telora, so is our first ancestor led by the mightiest telora whose name is Itheran."

The thought was that these telora were spirit beings of some kind. David's mind revolted against accepting this, but as he understood it from the man's thoughts, they were simply created beings of great intellect, moving in an entirely different dimension but able to enter at least one other dimension at will.

"Do these telora oppress your people?"

David could tell that his thought was foreign to his host so that he could not really reply. "Ruler" was not a clear concept to him, for it implies rule by force and power, and although David sensed an immense awe in the mind of this creature toward the telora, apparently everyone happily followed their guidance because this was the natural way to pleasures and fulfillment.

"And so Itheran is the ultimate?" David asked. "He rules in your world and worlds and in mine as well?"

The man's face contorted in bewilderment at David. It was obviously an unthinkable thought, as unthinkable as if David had just denied his own existence. That the earthling could be so uninformed about the ruler of his own world was a strange revelation.

"Itheran is leader of our worlds only. Your galaxies—antimatter—are ruled by the Twisted One. But he was made. And I was made. And Itheran was made. We are all made."

"By whom?"

"Aelor!"

At the mention of this name, David sensed in the mind of the creature a very complex concept, yet very real, as if Aelor were part of his being. His thoughts, however, were not pantheistic. The awe toward Aelor in the active brain was far too much for David to comprehend. He could not bear the immensity of the concepts, and noting the discomfiture of the earthling, the creature desisted.

Then David's host sat for a time, going into communication

again as if held in a trance. After a short time he rose, then led David to the room in which he had been originally examined. Looking through the porthole, David realized the craft was once again in the air, above land.

Suddenly, without a thought of warning, the floor gave way and to his horror David was catapulted out, screaming, into the cold air above the clouds. With stomach-wrenching turns, he flattened himself out in the air like a sky diver, desperately trying to slow his descent but picking up more and more speed.

David tried to tell himself that he would be picked up by the craft somehow. Yet he doubted it. After the initial frenzy, he retained a constant speed in his rush toward earth.

There was no ripcord to pull. Suddenly the fluffy white clouds below disappeared, and fields and houses rushed up as if the entire countryside were being shot at him. He began to black out. Then his whole body seemed pressured by a strange force, and he knew nothing more.

3

David had awakened not far from his car, morning light warming his face. He had risen and found himself quite well, his keys in his pocket. And he had soon found his car engine quite willing to start.

He was too close to the experience to begin immediately thinking it had been fantasy. But as he drove toward home that morning the explanation gradually grew on him. Could it not have been a dream—or a nightmare? He had seen a bright light, true, and had left his car to investigate, but then could he not have fallen and hit his head? He reasoned that the reality of such a dream can be strong, and that it could easily have been shaped by the numerous UFO reports and articles resulting from the local wave of sightings.

Charlotte had been at home when he arrived. She was a senior at the university, but had not gone to class that morning. As soon as he stepped in the front door, she was there, asking, "Where have you been? As soon as I woke up, and you weren't here, I started calling and looking all over the house. *What in the world* happened?"

She said it kindly, watching his distraught eyes.

"Something crazy," he explained, staring blankly at the wall. "A wild, unbelievable dream that never ended till an hour ago."

He started with the bright light on the highway. "I suppose it was the UFO people have been sighting around here—aircraft or test rocket or who knows what. My engine died almost as soon as I sighted it. I couldn't start it again, so I pushed it off the road.

"The light was distinct before me, and I wanted to get a look at it—so I started out across the field toward it."

Here he paused, his mind playing with the scenes which came next, wanting to reject their reality. Keeping his eyes from her face, he continued, "It must have been as I was running across that field that I slipped or something, for I had the wildest dream. Maybe even whatever caused my engine to die caused some kind of shock to my system and put me into a fever or something."

He looked over at her. "Want to hear the dream?"

She nodded.

"It's straight out of H. G. Wells—but here goes!"

It took him more than an hour to recount the whole thing and answer her questions. Charlotte watched his face as he talked, but didn't reveal her own thoughts.

"Of course, it *had* to be a dream." He smiled. "I wake up right by my car. I fall out of a space ship and never hit bottom . . . which is the classic dream, fall off cliffs and buildings, you know. They say if you hit while you're dreaming you never wake up . . . ."

Charlotte smiled with him and agreed. It was not so much David's story which bothered her—it was his attitude toward it, and the deep uneasiness in him. The quote from a class flitted across her mind that the more intelligent one is, the closer he is to insanity. David, she knew, was very intelligent. He was also an emotional, visceral young man.

They sat in silence for some time, but finally looked at the clock, and gulped down a hasty breakfast of cereal and toast.

"I gotta get going," David grunted, crunching down a last piece of marmalade toast, then a final cup of coffee. He felt into his pants pocket for his car keys, and as he grabbed them, his fingers also fished up a piece of heavy paper.

He pulled it out, and Charlotte watched him as he looked at it. Almost metallic, blue, it was instantly familiar to David.

His stomach churned. Spelled out by machine on the paper were figures something like ·III·III·III and >I·III·III·III.

They were perfectly analogous to 17,000,000,000 and 10,-000,000,000, and it appeared identical to the printout from the machine the humanoid had used to compute the distance to his home.

Charlotte was very much aware of his physical reaction on noticing the paper. She took it from him and studied it carefully. She, too, remembered the printout part of David's story.

They stood there for a moment. Dry-mouthed, he took the paper back from her and commented, "Must have picked this up somewhere . . . and it appeared in the dream. You know how it works in dreams. Alarm clocks correspond to school bells. Covers falling off puts you into a cold, snowy dream."

She nodded agreement.

He kissed her good-bye and rushed out the door to his car. But he felt a panic creeping in. He couldn't imagine where he could have gotten a paper like this—so unique—without remembering it. The panic was completely different from the one he had felt on facing death just hours before. That had been a clear, cold panic shooting adrenalin into the bloodstream and making him do whatever necessary to preserve himself. But this was a muddy, unreasoning panic. Either the experience had been real last night, or he was having a psychotic dream. Just the thought of his mind's proving untrustworthy was appalling. He had seen intelligent college students reduced to dull-eyed depressives in state institutions. Nothing could be more personally horrifying than that.

The reality of the experience was hard to dismiss. Could it

be that some anti-gravity principle had eased his impact on falling from the ship? Maybe the humanoid had not been aware of the agony David would go through in falling and in meeting the force which so quickly blacked him out. In fact, maybe the humanoid was not even acquainted with pain. Had he evolved to the point where in his safe world pain—simply messages of danger to the control center—was unnecessary and, therefore, eliminated? It had seemed that the humanoid had had no understanding of it when David had conveyed fears and strong feelings of discomfort.

* * *

Ten days later, David sat in his assistant public relations cubicle typing captions for pictures of a new singing group. His boss, George Phelps, emerged from the office across the hall, lips set tight. He motioned David into his office. Immediately, a copy of *Hit Sixteen* magazine was rammed into his hands.

"Thanks a *lot!*" Phelps blasted, bending the pages into view which showed a full spread on The Union Jacks.

"They printed my story," David responded, bewildered at Phelps' attitude. "Publicity. Free. That's what our job's all about. What's the beef?"

"Look, you idiot! The public relations arm of Arco does not send out stories on its own recording stars that tear them apart!" Phelps sat down and tipped back his chair, glaring at his assistant.

"Realism!" David retorted. "That's why they printed it. So I said the Jacks were off base on a couple songs, that they shouldn't belch up the gutter if they expect to keep the respect of today's kids. Well, some teens will respond to that kind of writing and reject them—but most will ignore it anyway, and you get the free publicity."

"*We* get publicity? This is *your* job, too, Koehler. And just because you've got a fourteen-year-old sister back at the farm doesn't mean you have to censor the world's pop music for her. You're acting like an idiot!"

Fire exploded into David's neck muscles and face. He glared back at Phelps. "O.K., so I have a little sister, and she's only fourteen. Yes, that's *exactly* right, and I don't want some cruddy leeches like the Jacks singing *this* to her!" David picked up the record from Phelps' desk, put it on the turntable and selected the song. A hammering beat with a great variety of background accompaniment almost overpowered the voice which wove in with the words:

> *Face, you've got a face, luv,*
> > *and I want you to be mine*
> *Face that's so lovely*
> > *it's too much, too much, luv . . . .*

Drums hammered away and drowned out the voice which then reappeared:

> *Hair, you've got hair, luv,*
> > *and I want you to be mine*
> *Hair that's so lovely,*
> > *it's to touch, to touch, luv . . . .*

Again the drums and strings drowned him out in a beating rock. Then:

> *Soft, you are soft, luv,*
> > *and I want you to be mine*
> *Soft, that's so lovely,*
> > *it's to touch, to touch, luv . . . .*

BUT YOU AIN'T MINE, YOU AIN'T MINE, YOU AIN'T MINE, MY LUV,
(the beat was intensifying)
> *You're a woman, but you ain't mine cause you're*
> *still a little girl!*

A sudden change of pace, the music lilted into a circusy lollipops-and-candy children's tune, and the singer taunted from way in the background,

> *You're a little girl who's grown up*
> > *and you don't know what to do*
> *You're a little girl who tells me*
> > *it ain't right, it ain't right*
> *—so I'll hold you when you grow up, little—*

Suddenly, as if in mid-sentence, the song finished.

"*Sure* I've got a sister," David repeated, fingering the record jacket. "And she'll listen to this 'cause it's on the Arco label, and she knows I work for Arco. Now don't pigeonhole me! I've got nothing against love and happiness and sex and let's all go out and have an orgy. But I don't like these pressure tactics on *kids* . . . telling a junior-high girl she's got a woman's body and a child's outlook and she'll lose her boyfriend if she doesn't go to bed with him. You *know* that's what the Jacks mean. So, neat! She gets pregnant before she's out of the eighth grade! Now, *that's* where I draw the line. You know it's junior-high girls who listen to this stuff!"

Phelps was watching him with a steely expression, and drilled in with, "Tell it to The Union Jacks—not me, not the magazine editors of the world, not the paying customers of our products. If you don't like the music here, go plug Julie Andrews!"

They glared at each other for a few moments, then David twisted around and returned to his desk. Carla Adams, the PR secretary, fortyish but graying, caught his eye and registered her approval of his speech by her sympathetic expression.

Unable to concentrate, he threw his work into a briefcase and strode out to his car. He drove around a while, trying to cool off.

It was almost at the precise spot on the road where he had seen the UFO that his engine died *again*. He was just able to guide his car to the shoulder of the road before he blacked out.

The next thing he knew, bizarre as it seemed, he found himself in the living room of the bronze man's spacecraft, with all the contents of his car spaced around him exactly as they had been positioned—jack and wrench behind him, glove compartment contents to his right, briefcase behind him.

The bronze man stood before him—immense and muscular, with his striking, metallic-specked skin and piercing azure eyes, more impressive than ever. The shock of finding himself back here started David's fears and frustrations pouring through his veins like sticky, molten metal.

Facing the man, he demanded: "What's this all about? Why did you bring me here?"

The bronze man smiled amiably and held out a *Time* magazine. "You left this," he said in perfect English. "It was in your coat pocket."

The vocalizing instead of thought projection startled David, and since the man didn't immediately supply an answer, he asked, "How can you speak to me—in my own language? Before you could communicate only directly to my mind."

The man smiled again. "I taped your conversations, even your dreams. I suppose you could best understand the process as 'physiological assimilation.' I absorbed your vocabulary and innuendos of accent. Frankly," he said, pausing a moment, "my greatest difficulty was keeping language separate from your attitudes and feelings, for I had been told that to assimilate this would be against Aelor's will."

"Why didn't you simply continue to use brain waves?"

"Because you are more comfortable if we simply talk."

David looked at the *Time* magazine. He had wondered where his copy had gotten to. "You can read this now?" David asked.

The man simply nodded.

They sat there for some time, neither speaking but both observing one another. "What is your name?" David asked finally.

"I could not put the sounds of it into your language. But it would be closest to this: 'Pélu.' "

The bronze man picked up the magazine, paused again, then said in a mystified tone of voice, "Why do your writers dwell so on things that are not? Do all these fantasies help you appreciate reality? They are so . . . uh, unfortunate, unhappy."

Although the creature was projecting his thoughts in an effort to get his meaning across, David could not catch what he was driving at.

"Here!" Pélu stood, and stooped over to show him a photo of a black man chained to a tree so grotesquely that his back looked broken. The text described the incident, then indicated the scores of lynchings per year in the United States in the first half of the century.

"And here . . ." The man turned to an article on divorce and society's attempts to cope with the problem.

Pélu was using all the power of his magnificent intellect to drive into David's brain the unbelievable strangeness of all this from his point of view. "Why would earth's writers develop such strange fictions, for even in this Hurt World, surely this is the thing that is not."

The force of Pélu's intellect and point of view became increasingly clear to David, for he could see the absurdity of it all through the creature's mind.

"No, Pélu. What you read is factual. It is life here."

They were silent for a few moments. Then David demanded, "Why did you come here anyway? You told me that you were forbidden to listen to any of this on your radios or equipment, and that you could make no contact."

The man stood and leaned back against the wall. "Because we have a mission here—against the twisted telora."

David's mind immediately came back to thoughts of espionage. Why couldn't this man be part of some military establishment on earth? Why couldn't he be a Russian infiltrator with technology beyond what Americans thought them capable of? In fact, could this not be some incredible hoax through hypnotism or some manipulation of the mind? Could the ship, the entire surroundings, be in his mind—placed there by hypno-suggestion?

"Who *is* your leader?" David demanded.

"Aelor," was the answer. Pélu looked perplexed. "I have told you this. Whose is He not?"

They were reading each other's thoughts again, and David perceived the full reality of how unthinkable it was to Pélu that he could be in allegiance to anyone but Aelor. Yet even as he absorbed this concept, David further reasoned—if this man reads minds, could he not manipulate mine so that I would be thinking he was thinking something he was not? Why *couldn't* he be a Russian? It would make so much sense!

David's idea further bewildered the man, and he blazed, "Your mind is so . . . so . . . to use your word, devious. Do you have no contact yourself with Aelor?"

"No. None at all," David said definitely.

"But you live in Aelor. You breathe in Aelor." Pélu sat down again and said, forcefully and clearly, "You then, David, are cut off from reality."

Thoughts caromed off every corner of David's brain as he tried to piece it all together. If Pélu were an alien, had he evolved to some kind of advanced pantheism? Was he truly so close to the center of creation that he did know something about the ultimate causes?

Or was this man a human, bent on using him somehow? Was it all like a magic show of startling new scientific advances? Maybe Pélu was quite devious himself, quite capable of pain.

Suddenly, David whipped around and struck him hard across the face, careful to hit the nose as well as the cheek.

The big bronze man's head snapped back. He stared at David, his face blank of expression. No tears were welling in his eyes, though his cheeks were reddening, and a scratch from David's ring was filling with little spots of blood.

David slumped and mumbled, "Sorry. *Really*—I'm sorry. It was a test . . . a search for truth."

The man shrugged—in the same manner David once had on the spaceship—and sat down beside him.

For the rest of that afternoon David's questions centered on such things as anti-gravity and thought projection, whereas the visitor asked more sociological questions. A strange rapport began to build between them. David could not help but appreciate the man's gentle but brilliant personality.

Pélu quizzed him about the books and magazines which were in his briefcase and car. "I can take only a few minutes at a time of reading them," Pélu commented, "then I must get back to reality." He rose and knitted his brows. "Tell me, David, where is Aelor in this world? I read various names which are worshiped. Are these your names for Aelor? If so, the symbolism hardly fits!"

"But what is Aelor?" David interrupted. "If he is the ultimate cause in your world—"

"He *is!*" Pélu declared, pouring his thoughts into David's mind. Yet neither the words nor thoughts could convey the meaning, the awe, David could feel Pélu had toward the overwhelming magnificence of his supreme commander. Yet Aelor was far, far beyond defining, for only a little of the concept's immensity in Pélu's brain was filtering down to the earthling's mind—and they both knew it.

Pélu sat pensively across from David, his visage changed somewhat from the first time he had seen him. His was more than a learning experience in a new culture. It was as if innocence had come to grips with evil for the first time.

"How can it be?" Pélu asked, those azure eyes boring into David's. He seated himself in the soft blue of the living area. They were silent for a lengthy time. "We were always told," the powerful bronze man mused, as if piecing things together in his own mind, "that here in the vastness of Zoir—that is, the void of antimatter—great conflicts were going on. We have been told, too, of a great telora—a ruler of thousands of worlds—who was cast here because he had tried to usurp the place of Aelor and became twisted. Always we knew that the greatest dramas, the most magnificent conflicts in all of creation, were occurring here.

"But no matter how we might have dreamed, never could our brains have conjured up so disrupted, so shuddering a chaos as your only inhabited planet of Zoir—this earth of killing, hatreds, absence of love."

David watched him closely, trying desperately to piece it all together. He was filled with wonder at the creature, and felt a deep awe. Yet at the same time he resented the bluntness of the man and the personal implications. He felt compelled to attack the prejudice Pélu obviously had against a culture different from his own. "Love!" David rebutted, standing to his feet. "How can you say we have no love? Search out the feelings between Charlotte and me. If you could only know how they've grown! And our love must be pitted against the sharp, jagged environment in which we live. Maybe your love can exceed ours because you can give it constantly. But you've experienced no frustrations. Your body doesn't know pain. You don't have the terrible pressures of loneliness, of fear— or hate. You don't have sorrow, compulsions, insecurity, and all the emotions necessary from the time of our primitive ancestors to stay alive."

"You are wrong!" Pélu corrected him immediately. The authority in his voice chilled David and at the same time angered him further. "I do not understand these emotions on earth or why you have them. But they are not necessary for survival, even if you and your woman were starting out alone on your planet to conquer it and people it—no matter how hostile your world. These emotions are twisted. They ruin you and tear down your world. If you delete them, by now you would have conquered your solar system and far, far—"

"How could we?" David interrupted irritably. "Our neighboring planets have no atmosphere that would sustain us."

"It takes little creativity to provide your own! But your love. It's completely different from our love in Selansé, my planet. Your books and magazines show earth love as streaked with selfishness. Your love for Charlotte, from your own thoughts, is only fulfilling your needs of coping with insecurity and loneliness. Your love is primarily a response to what she can do for you to fill your needs, as you would respond to a new vehicle or to food."

"So what's wrong with that?" David demanded.

"Nothing. Except that it's all centrifugal, all centering on yourself, dwarfing you. We too have emotions—desire to become one and be together—but not fears of loneliness and insecurity. Our love is in joining together in Aelor to fulfill each other's joy in sharing in his creativity. Remember, Aelor could have created your planet and my planet complete. He could have made gleaming cities and completed airways—a planet equipped as you and I could not conceive. But he allowed us to share in his creativity to build, to level, to create, to explore, to pioneer, to join with another, to raise children, to conquer—all with his love in us. But your love is bent. Something is terribly wrong. You live only a few years. You kill. You love, but love turns to hate."

David felt like a fool arguing against someone of such intellect. Yet the ideas were so unacceptable he almost felt he was fighting for his sanity, for his self-worth as a rational being. He disliked the arrogance of a man—no matter how advanced—who could flatly say David's love was selfish and in the same breath extol his own love. "I don't buy it!" he declared. "Your technological superiority and your advancement on the evolutionary scale give you no right to sneer at those of us who are going through the primordial throes of starting a civilization. Your own ancestors millions of years ago probably lived the same way. *You're* the one who's in decline. You've conquered pain and fear and hatreds because you've conquered your worlds, so now you'll probably degenerate into meaningless, directionless organisms ready for destruction and a new trillion-year cycle. I don't deny your advancement, or your happier state free from our struggles, but don't sneer at us!"

The creature from beyond the quasars stared at the earthling and finally pursed his lips as if hearing the most monstrous of absurdities. "David, my friend. If you could see how these emotions are like poisons to your organisms. They are not natural evolvement. They are devolvement. They tear you apart. I only marvel that without Aelor you have even come this far in your world."

"Aelor, whoever he is, lives in your world. Not this one. And he didn't make this planet!"

"He made it," Pélu insisted. "He made all. But the twisted telora who rules your world holds you from him."

David stretched himself out on the lower plateau. It was impossibly weird, talking like this to a creature from another world, in a spacecraft. It had to be some absurd fantasy.

He felt the authority of the creature. Yet why should he feel that inferior? "You sound like an Irishman talking about leprechauns and forests," David accused. "You keep telling me about Aelor being here, but he isn't. He made it, but he doesn't run it, but telora who are bad do. How do you know our culture isn't more normal than yours? Maybe our depth of experience is of greater value than a hot-house life of the ultimate in scientific and biological refinement!"

Pélu shook his head. "If you could spend just *one day* on my planet and know its joys and delights. But here—this world pulls its atmosphere over me like a putrid black cloud.

"How can I describe it to you?" Pélu demanded, using the full force of his mind to pour into the earthling his thought, emotions, and perspective. "It is like coming to a black hole in the earth and peering down . . . then climbing in and suddenly falling, through blackness and vile smells and putrifying filth.

"I remind you, David, that I use these words 'vile' and 'filth' because they are your words and belong only in this vastness of antimatter. In my four thousand years of life, I had never before known such concepts. Even in you and in all I meet, there is the smell of death, of unwholeness, of twisted minds and bodies, dwarfed from your real selves.

"There is a force here—a gigantic force. It is the enemy of Aelor.

"How else?" he asked. "How else do you explain not only your own bickering and fighting, but *this!*"

He held open an old magazine article about two convicted killers in England. "David, this man and woman took little children onto these moors to torture them, tearing their flesh and recording their screams—and *enjoying* it!

"I admit I do not understand pain. But I have read. And I have observed you. It is unbelievable that even pain itself could exist—that Aelor would not dissolve it. But for humans to inflict pain on their own and derive pleasure!"

"Demented," David quietly agreed, gritting his teeth. "Too horrible to even conceive."

Pélu's eyes darted to a direct stare into David's own. "But I must tell you the thing that is. I detect the same potential in even you, my friend. That desire to hurt, even to kill, to use words to slice at a person's chest and mind, to push yourself up and derive pleasure from standing on them or seeing them hurt."

Pélu paused again. "Your book quotes a psychiatrist as saying that these people who suddenly murder everyone in sight are possessed by an evil power beyond themselves, that it controls them . . . that one in every thousand of your people could suddenly do this.

"How can your planet let these people breathe? Why does not your world move them to the next—to the Twisted One's plane where they must belong?"

"You say we're all that way," David supplied, with a touch of sarcasm but deeper fear growing within.

Pélu listened and evaluated, "Yes, you are. That is what appalls me about your attitude toward it all. As if it were normal."

Pélu picked up another magazine article, and David could see a hot fury building, hotter than when he was talking of sadism and pain.

"How can this thing be?" he demanded! "This sentence—'Russian landowners reserved the right to sleep with the bride the first night of his peasant's marriage.' And here," he turned the page, "it talks of white men 'buying' black men and using their women to satisfy what you call lust!" David sensed from his thoughts that Pélu's oneness with his own lover made this too incredible to comprehend, something destroying the very fabric of life itself.

His indignation was like a boiling sun casting out purging rays, and David couldn't absorb all the thoughts and emotions being driven directly into his mind.

4

Carla Adams, the senior public relations secretary from Arco, was with Charlotte at a small corner table in the Golden Moon Restaurant eating ham sandwiches made with the specialty of the house: very dark, thick rye bread.

"It's happened twice now," Charlotte was saying. "He's come home after being out all night in a wild adventure or dream or whatever's happening, wild-eyed and distraught. How am I *supposed* to take it? Hold his hand? Rush him off to a clinic? Probe and pry?"

"Who knows?" Carla responded. "He told me, too, this last time . . . and I so much wanted to help, but when you don't even know what in the world actually happened, how *can* you?"

"If it happens again," Charlotte said, grimacing, "I swear I'm going to have my psych prof out for dinner and have David explain it all to *him*!"

"Maybe so . . . but what if this thing is real somehow— even a weird hoax?"

They sat in silence eating the dark rye and sipping coffee. Finally, as they were about to leave, Carla unobstrusively picked up the check, then with firm emphasis cautioned,

"Whatever happens, Charlotte, don't let it become a wedge to split you two up. If ever he needs you, it's *now,* and you know very well that it's what *you* do that can make or break the guy. And you know me well enough to know I'm not just throwing all the responsibility on you, but pleading for you to do what maybe a lot of brides *couldn't.* You know what I mean: a human is fragile in a lot of ways, and you're the key to keeping David together."

Charlotte didn't answer—although she had her own opinions—but she thanked Carla for the lunch, then took the city bus to her mother's home for the afternoon visit she had promised.

Charlotte had also promised herself she would share the whole situation with her mother. She *had* to—she never did hide anything from her. The fact was, her mother was often nearly obsequious in trying to keep Charlotte's favor.

After nearly an hour of chatter, then lengthy discussion about David and the UFO, mother and daughter had gone into Charlotte's old bedroom for a blouse she wanted, and ended up sitting on her bed. The mother was talking about how quickly time had flown, how things had changed, how maybe before too long she and David might be having a baby and she'd become a grandmother.

Charlotte felt the eyes of her mother reaching out and hungering for her love, absorbing her, clinging to her, wanting her never to leave. Charlotte felt stifled, as she always did at this, yet at the same time wanted to reach out to her also.

"It may not be *too* long before we have one . . . but first I have to get out of college. . . ."

"You don't think you'll be moving away after that, do you?" the mother asked, trying to keep the concern out of her voice.

"Oh, I doubt that very much!" Charlotte replied.

There was silence between them for a time. Then the mother sat down on the corner of the bed, staring at a baby photo of Charlotte which stood on the ornate ivory colored dresser. "It'll be so wonderful to hold your little baby. One thing you sure won't have to pay for," she smiled uneasily, "is baby-sitters." She paused, and looked up. "Oh, but I won't be possessive. You know that!"

"Mom," Charlotte assured, "just talk about it. Go ahead."

Her mother kept staring at the picture. "How can I describe how it feels to hold a three-months-old baby in your arms? Little Barbara. My very own loving baby, cute and precious. But now she's dead. One moment alive, the next . . . the smile, the little arms, all warm and seeming alive. But no heartbeat.

"Then it was two years later we had a new Barbara. A year old—a whole year old, and so cute and active and lively. And then that day when she was dead, too. So impossible. But she was."

The mother stopped talking. Charlotte watched her lips rubbing back and forth against each other. Then: "We couldn't name *you* Barbara. We just couldn't. Now I can still hold you alive. You're the *only* one."

There was loving communication between them now, and the mother did not have to say how she had also held her husband in her arms at four o'clock one morning two years ago, dying of a heart attack. And he having been worse than dead for the ten years before that, with a slowly growing lunacy which eventually became such that it should have been contained in an institution. But it was contained in the body of a man Charlotte's mother had loved, had protected, and now still missed very much.

Charlotte felt a similar touch of the massive hunger her mother felt for her rising in her own breast. She felt, too, a taste of the fear she knew her mother was trying to communicate about David's strange actions. Her mother was terrified by it all, whatever it meant.

And Charlotte, who had lived those full ten years of anguish with her father, was not particularly objective about it herself.

*   *   *

David and Charlotte's tiny rented home was about ten miles from the city of 100,000 where they worked and studied. The suburban sprawl had not overtaken the rolling mountains near their home, and David loved to escape the tensions by walking through the woods and fields.

He felt especially tense now, and even as Charlotte was speaking to her mother, he was walking along the faint old wagon trails and past the wide, flattened stone rows.

(46)

He hungered, almost in a physical way, for reality, for old moorings of simple ideas and the rich earth and the toil of men with character. The strangeness of his experiences tore him from the simplicities.

David adjusted the target pistol on his hip—an old H. & R. .22 he always carried as he walked. Clouds above spread themselves lazily against the blue sky, forming grotesque patterns which his imagination changed into faces and animals. Shafts of sunlight streaked past the foliage and greedily sucked up sparkling drops of moisture.

David walked up to one of the stone rows which rambled obdurately but irregularly along the one-time fields, as if to mock the vanishing trails. He stooped at one of the gray, uneven piles and picked up a long, shale-like piece.

I wonder who it was, he thought, *who threw this here a hundred years ago to make a field. Now his field is woods again, his farm is woods again, and the rocks are mute gray tombstones to mark his sweat and toil. Yet how permanent he must have felt, and now no one even knows who he was. He's somewhere in a different plane now.*

He turned away, flipping the rock back. *Some day, I suppose, someone will be fingering the rocks I've strewn around, and care as little.*

Hawks, etched black against the sky, glided with the wind as it buffeted them up and down. He watched as they dipped, like a squadron of reconnaissance planes. They drew him to walk up the hill.

It was steep going for about twenty minutes, and he was out of breath when he reached the top. Turning and looking down, he saw irregular squares of brown and yellow dotted with tiny white houses and ponds and a skinny brown road squirming around them. Hazy, blue hills in the distance seemed to be reaching and rolling up to the fields below, and the sky in the distance almost merged with the mountains.

A car, small and insignificant, weaved up to one of the toy houses and stopped. He stared at it. From this perspective, he felt tiny and insignificant himself.

The clouds darkened and the temperature started dropping. David reluctantly began the descent, but before he was halfway down, drizzling rain dampened his face and clothes.

He walked more briskly, ducking under the big oaks and smaller poplars. The drizzle was in his eyes, and he almost began to run . . . when he noticed a figure under a big scotch pine. Tall and erect, the figure stood as if watching him intently, oblivious to the precipitation.

The drizzle turned to light rain, and the wetness increased the chill spreading across his back. He stared at the figure, and David could see now that the clothes he wore were identical to what he himself had worn last time he had been aboard the spacecraft—except these fit the larger man perfectly. And the more he stared at the distant figure, the more he realized how bronze the face looked, almost a metallic quality, with a faint shimmer.

The figure stepped from under the tree and walked toward him, great distance-eating steps, and David wondered if he should not change his course and avoid him if at all possible. Now that he saw Pélu again he wanted no part of all this. He wanted to be freed from it, and if this man were now to invade his own world, walk around in it. . . .

David shrank back against the trunk of a huge oak and waited as the figure approached. He could see now that the face was stern, that something cataclysmic had happened, that he was intent on David's face.

Finally, he stood before him, just beyond the protection of the oak leaves, oblivious to the rain dripping from his face, staring at David and obviously churning inside with emotions —possibly, David thought, emotions he had never experienced before in his thousands of years.

The bronze figure said nothing for a full minute. Then he accused with a steely voice: "You have murdered him!"

David's brow immediately knit together, and he clenched his teeth. "Who?" he demanded, keeping his eyes on his.

The humanoid said the next word with hushed unbelievability in his voice.

"Aelor!"

David started in bewilderment. What kind of an aberration was this? He tried desperately to collect his thoughts. "You told me Aelor is in your world, the maker of trillions of worlds and dimensions and beings. And I would die if I but saw him. And you accuse me of being his killer?"

"You," Pélu declared with finality, "and your race. You laid open his back with leaded whips. You hated him. You drove him to exhaustion, then you slowly butchered him like an animal for slaughter. Aelor-ké—the heir himself—you tortured and hanged up—"

Pélu stopped in mid-sentence, and simply stared at the earthling. David wondered if the extreme shock of first confronting such things as cruelty and pain had so tormented the man's great mind that it had snapped.

"If Aelor can make worlds, surely he can defend himself," David said slowly. "Why didn't he kill us?"

Pélu didn't answer for several minutes. He simply stared at David, seemingly wanting the enormity of this to sink into the earthling's consciousness. Finally, "He could have. His very being is such blinding, purifying light that created beings would be consumed. But he came as an offspring of your race. It's more than my mind—any mind—can grasp. He pushed aside all powers, the least of which could destroy or create a world.

"It was as if you, David, were to become a maggot, and wallow with them in their filth. Aelor shed his magnificence to walk in the corruption of this planet . . . and—you killed him."

The bronze visitor's face was contorted with emotion. "For the first time," he said, "I believe I know something of this thing you call pain."

David stood there quietly, fearful of the powerful man with such intensity and bizarre statements. He leaned back against the dripping oak, never taking his eyes from those of his visitor.

Pélu continued to stare for several minutes. Then—"I said it that way, David, so you could see at least a ray of the enormity of what has been done."

David continued staring, thinking, fearing.

"I obtained a Bible two days ago," Pélu explained. "It has the entire story of—"

David shut his eyes hard and wanted to scream and laugh and shout at the man all at once. But the only thing that came out was a nervous, almost coughing little laugh with the words, "Surely, just because you read those stories about Jesus doesn't mean he was your Aelor. Jesus Christ was a religious young Jew who was executed a couple thousand years ago."

Pélu smiled—that maddening smile, as if he were teaching

a child—and said, "Don't you know that Jesus said, 'I and my father are one'? That is *why* they killed him. He made himself equal with Aelor!"

"I know, I know," David said impatiently. "Jesus made all sorts of claims, and Christians believe He is God, second person of the Trinity—whoever God may be. But you don't just accept ancient fables handed down from generation to generation handwritten. These are old manuscripts and interpretations of superstitious monks from the Middle Ages."

"You cannot find truth simply through your intellect," Pélu responded.

"Am I to discard my mind? That reduces me to a babbling child."

"Well," Pélu rejoined, "isn't that what you are now?"

Nothing the bronzed man had said since their first meeting had angered David quite as much as that quick remark. "What do you mean?" he demanded curtly.

"Analyze yourself. You accept or reject on the basis of who is the most eloquent speaker. You make decisions not knowing every detail. Most presentations are biased—and you become biased. It's like being the judge of a debate. You choose the winning side. But you well know that the winning side may have presented the incorrect view. Persuasion and presentation won—not truth." Pélu smiled at him. "There are certain absolute lies you believe right now which you would fight for to the end!"

He waited for David's reaction, but he did not respond. Pélu then added, "Doesn't it seem necessary to have another force to guide your mind into truth—a yielding to the omniscience of Aelor? On this planet, everyone holds diametrically opposed beliefs on subjects. Obviously, many are wrong. If Aelor were guiding their thinking, they would know truth."

"Pélu, it surprises me," David said, "that you read this book, the Bible, and just accept it. I could have given you the Koran or any one of hundreds of like books with similar fantasies. You—"

"No," Pélu interrupted. "Aelor *does guide* my mind. I have direct communication with him—as you could have."

David shivered from the wetness and hunched his shoulders under his jacket. It was all so absurd, standing here in this

(50)

rain like part of an Edgar Allen Poe dream of monstrous visions and colors. Yet this Pélu was so awesome in his assurance of truth.

"As your Bible says," Pélu continued, "your creation here is like a woman in the intense pain of childbirth. *Nothing* is normal. All awaits a new day. Before I read this book, I thought the planet was utterly hopeless, that your pain would go on and on. But you are in warfare—and Aelor will win."

He watched Pélu standing there in the rain. Why was all this happening to *him?* "There are horrors, atrocities, true," David intoned deliberately, fighting to make sense, "but this is the way of our planet—to keep the population in check. I've never heard a religionist say that animals are 'evil,' yet they fight for territorial rights. They kill. They steal. They even eat their own kind!"

Pélu's manner showed an impatience with this immediately negative response, as if David were an unborn baby resisting the inevitability of being cast from his mother's womb. "It is incredible that you think of yourself as just an animal. A man is not twisted because he kills or usurps, nor even because he eats his own people, but because he was made to have the Aelor-force flowing through him, and he rejects it. His rejection means he lives like an animal, not like Aelor in whose image he was made. God gave laws in your Bible. You break them. It shows how you live without Aelor flowing through you."

David felt boxed in, pressured. He moved forward and stared at Pélu.

"Why did you come?" he exploded. "Why did you come to *me!* Out of all the billions of humans, why torture *my* brain? Why must I be the one to judge if you are a rational being or a creature from an insane world that grasps at fantasies. Why me?" he yelled, standing and pounding his fist into his open palm.

"Because," Pélu said in a level, constrained voice, "Aelor has a special plan for you and me against the twisted ones. But you can reject it, as your race usually does. I can't force you to reality if you want the twisted ones to control you."

"Koehler!"

The shout came from the left, and David looked there to

see, about thirty yards off, the figure of Phelps advancing warily and glancing not only at him and Pélu, but at three companions who were advancing stealthily, each from a different direction.

Phelps' boots crunched heavily on the oak leaves as he came up to the pair. David's eyes darted to his companion, assessing what these men must be thinking. Pélu looked rather natural standing there in David's stylish type of clothes, his hand resting carelessly in his pocket. Yet his skin was obviously unlike anything they had ever seen before. The rain had stopped, and in the wide rays of sunshine the reflections from the bronze flecks of his skin sparkled like a newly hammered shield. He was seven feet tall. His face, too, was unmistakably unique. The smaller nose, V-shaped chin, piercing, wide-set eyes—with eyebrows and straight hair of an almost metallic-gold texture—combined to make him strikingly attractive and acceptable, but hardly the kind of person you'd expect to meet while wandering around the Pennsylvania countryside.

David recognized the men with Phelps. They were all from the office—writers and photographers. In fact, one was already clicking away with his camera aimed at Pélu.

"We all sensed something was up," Phelps was saying, obviously in a high state of excitement, "with you acting so strangely. Thought it might have to do with all these UFO reports . . . aren't you going to introduce us to your friend?"

David did so, and from then on Pélu dominated the conversation, answering their questions candidly.

"Where are you from?" Phelps asked.

"Selansé—which is beyond your universe."

"You can't be beyond the *universe*—that's all there is—by definition."

Pélu smiled without irritation. "Well, beyond your quasars then, and beyond the range of anything you can detect. Millions of 'light years,' you know."

All the men looked flabbergasted at that, and David sensed that they were beginning to think this some kind of hoax. "And you came in a spaceship?" demanded the red-haired fat man with the tiny tape recorder.

"You would call it that."

Phelps fidgeted. "How many on your crew?"

"There is need for only one. Others of my race, on special command of Aelor, are also here in your universe, but each has his own ship. Of course, we may not be the only ones. The creatures and messengers of Aelor are infinite in number."

The strange traveler relaxed his back against the oak and smiled, as if he were enjoying the conversation, his eyes following their movements. The men were looking at each other, disbelieving, searching for a plan of action. David knew Pélu was reading their minds. Apparently, they did not.

The mention of Aelor intrigued the men, and one asked who and what he was. "The maker of universes and peoples, the one who formed me and mine, who made the crafts and our worlds with us and without us, who breathes in us and we in him. . . ."

"Where is your spaceship then?" the fat man demanded. "Let's go see it."

"No. It is in the ocean, and will travel by remote control when I desire it to."

The fat man averted his eyes and was clearly thinking unkind thoughts about the traveler.

"Why do you think I tell you what is not?" Pélu suddenly exploded. "You speak so nicely on the outside but on the inside each one of you thinks the thoughts which come from your twisted enemies." He turned his eyes to Phelps. "Right now you are trying to figure out ways to confine me so that you can take me to your own building so that you can use me to your ends. Gentlemen, I cannot but spend five minutes with you, and your thoughts are a jumble of deviousness which show your writings are ghastly—but accurate."

"But," Phelps protested, "all we've done is ask you some questions, and—"

"Good-bye," Pélu said suddenly, dismissing them all.

Miraculously, they obediently turned and walked away.

David looked over at his companion. "They will tell everyone, you know . . . and bring others."

"I doubt it," Pélu replied cooly. "They will remember nothing."

"But you saw him clicking that camera as he held it under his coat. And the fat one snapped on his tape recorder as he lighted his cigarette."

"Of course. Wrong chemicals will be used in developing the film. The other man will erase the tape. I've told them to."

He looked at David sternly. "Phelps—he is a pawn of the twisted telora to do hurt to your world . . . although he would deny it, even to himself. . . ."

At times David forgot his awe when he was with Pélu, but not now. He realized his magnificent advancement and his ability to concentrate his whole self on the matters at hand instead of fighting to control conflicting emotions and energies within. It was as if he lived, compared to musical scales, many octaves higher, with full ranges of emotions and drives and energies all within those octaves, but none of the lower base feelings which tear men apart. Only etched against Pélu's type of existence did earth's culture seem so barbaric, so dissonant.

"David," Pélu said, staring directly into his eyes, "I speak for your life or your death, and I do it that you might live."

He stooped, picked up a handful of oak leaves, and rubbed them between his palms. "You will be ground away like dust . . . you will soon be nothing but rotting flesh, and you know all this, yet you do not even try to find reality, to prepare for the next plane."

The earth man looked down at the thick bed of leaves below him, all curled and brown. "But no one has been beyond this plane—not even you. Believing fantasies won't prepare me."

Pélu never took his eyes off David's. "Have you never even *read* the statements by Jesus?" he asked sternly. 'I am going away; and you will search for me, and die in your sins. And you cannot come where I am going. . . . You are from below; I am from above. You are of this world; I am not. That is why I said that you will die in your sins, for unless you believe that I am the Messiah, the Son of God, you will die in your sins.' "

David watched Pélu, irritation growing. He'd heard second- and third-rate humans quoting this stuff, people who had never particularly impressed him. He wanted to be free from this whole strange adventure. And suddenly, he said just that to the towering bronze man.

Pélu answered nothing at first. Then he reached across to David and handed him a book. "You, then, need this far more than I. You will find I have marked some portions."

With that the bronze man walked off into the wooded fields.

*   *   *

That night, sitting in his den staring at the walls, David tried to come back to normalcy. Eyes closed or open, the ceiling spun in his mind with exotic swirlings of purples and reds and yellows, all mixing in his thoughts of fantastic worlds while religion reared a gargantuan body with a thousand heads. Most of all, an inner turmoil of opposing forces crashed against each other. It seemed that all the literature he'd ever read of the classic forces of good and evil in Everyman's life, of Milton and Shakespeare and Goethe, came for the first time into crisp clarity.

A black current of acidic liquid flowed through his organs and body telling him to get out, to take a drive, to get involved with something sane, to take Charlotte to a movie—anything.

If only he'd made Pélu come back with him to meet Charlotte, so she could understand, so that she could share the thing, so this would not be a wedge between them but something they could fight through together. Why hadn't he? *Why hadn't he?*

He wondered, too, if he shouldn't be going to the authorities. Who knew what in the world the implications of all this were, and what areas of national interest and security might be at stake?

He tried to lose himself in a James Bond novel, but even that high-powered fare couldn't command his concentration. Finally, he wandered out to the kitchen where Charlotte sat at the table, absorbed in her book on adolescent psychology. On seeing David at the door, she put a marker in her place and snapped it shut with a flourish.

"Saturday night. Time to pay a little attention to my man," she declared, bouncing up and over to him. She snuggled her face into his neck, and he played with her hair, stroking it along the curvature of her head and neck. The magic of holding each other was as potent, if not more so, as ever before. David felt almost hungry for her closeness, for her to blend with him in body and soul and to become a part of all he was and was tortured with.

He kissed her softly, then harder and harder . . . they stood there for long moments. holding each other tight in the magic of man and woman together.

Finally, she gave him a squeeze and moved over to the counter top. "Time to make you a little coffee," she announced. "Just you and me, coffee and oatmeal cookies, and we'll snuggle up by the TV and have our own twosome party . . . during the commercials."

She bustled around the kitchen and he sat there, responding to her small talk. It wasn't till much later, as they were embracing on the couch, that she asked in an offhanded manner, "Something happened this afternoon, didn't it? I could tell when I got home."

It turned him off, and he felt frustrated. She sensed it immediately and apologized for saying anything . . . "But why can't we talk about it?"

"'Cause I don't want to even *think* about it, much less talk about it. Anyway, I simply won't be having any of these experiences again. Whatever they were—dream, hoax, hypnotist. Click! I've turned it off. I've turned *him* off!"

Charlotte took his cue and changed the subject. She started talking about an aggressive "young turk" in her literature class who kept tearing down the prof's theses on Sartre. But neither David nor Charlotte could keep the conversation going, and they went to bed early.

It was at least an hour that David lay there, thoughts keeping his mind and body in a fully awake, agitated condition. He wanted very much to squeeze all those events right out of his brain, then relax his body and awake to a bright world next day. But it simply would not happen. And his curiosity about what Pélu might have marked in the Bible finally made him slip quietly from under the covers and feel his way through the dark to the kitchen where he had left it.

He groped for the light switch, clicked it, squinted his eyes against the brightness, then found the book.

It was a contemporary translation, and he flipped through the various sections—gospels, epistles, the Revelation. A long, thick piece of metal sticking out marked one section in Ephesians which had something written in the margin, next to a section completely encircled in deep black. The writing was the high-looped, thick foreslant Pélu used in imitation of David's handwriting.

David, it read, *these words from your book are my thoughts to Aelor for you. Read them very carefully.*

After looking at the note, a force within him warred against another force, one pushing him to snap it shut, to shove the book into the bookcase and "for God's sake, get some rest!" Yet the other force was saying that if Pélu were as brilliant and advanced as David knew him to be, and if he believed that Jesus was Aelor, then David was a fool not to investigate it.

More than anything else, curiosity made him read the encircled section, which was Ephesians 1:17-21:

"I pray for you constantly, asking God the glorious Father of our Lord Jesus Christ to give you wisdom to see clearly and really understand who Christ is and all He has done.

"I pray that your hearts will be flooded with light so that you can see something of the future He has called you to share. I want you to realize that God has been made rich because we who are Christ's have been given to Him!

"I pray that you will begin to understand how incredibly great His power is to help those who believe Him. It is that same mighty power

"That raised Christ from the dead and seated Him in the place of honor at God's right hand in heaven, Far, far above any other king or ruler or dictator or leader. Yes, His honor is far more glorious than that of any one else either in this world or in the world to come."

David stopped and sat thinking, staring. Finally, he reread it, slowly, thoughtfully.

Then he started flipping pages within this book of Ephesians and saw that it was quite short, so he went to the beginning of it to get it all in context. And even as he began to read, he sensed a fantastic drama going on in his own being, of the pull toward snapping the book shut and the opposite force drawing him into it.

It was late and his eyes were beginning to burn. He got up and put on some more coffee. Then he kept reading until he had finished all six of the little chapters, and he started at the beginning again and began to read it a second time.

Finally, trying to merge all this with the concepts Pélu had been throwing at him, he pulled out his felt-tipped marker and wrote in some headings over the verses which would parallel Pélu's statements.

Who is Jesus?

"The Psalmist tells about this, for he says that when Christ returned triumphantly to heaven after His resurrection and victory over Satan, He gave generous gifts to the children of men.

"Notice that it says He returned to heaven; this means that He had first come down from the heights of heaven, far down to the lowest parts of the earth. The same One who came down is the One who went back up, that He might be the ruler over all things everywhere, from the farthest down to the highest up."

Earth's people

"You went along with the crowd and were just like all the others, full of sin, obeying Satan, the mighty prince of the power of the air who is at work right now in the hearts of those who are against the Lord.

"Their closed hearts are full of darkness; they are far away from the life of God because they have shut their minds against Him, and they cannot understand His ways."

The Twisted Ones

"Put on all of God's armor so that you will be able to stand safe against the wiles of Satan. For we are not fighting against people made of flesh and blood, but against persons without bodies—the evil kings of the unseen world, those mighty satanic beings and great evil princes of darkness who rule this world; and against huge numbers of wicked spirits in the spirit world."

It excited David—reading all this. It was so different from what he'd imagined, and tied in so specifically and logically with what Pélu had been saying about all these things. "Now we can come fearlessly right into God's presence," David read, "assured of His glad welcome when we come with Christ and trust in Him." David thought of his being killed by a bullet in an Asian jungle, or hit by a car. After death, would it really be a "glad welcome"?

Pélu had also marked this section in the little epistle:

"When I think of the wisdom and scope of His plan I fall down on my knees and pray to the Father of all the great family of God—some of them up there in heaven and some down here on earth—that out of His glorious, unlimited resources He will give you the mighty inner strengthening of His Holy Spirit.

"And I pray that Christ will be more and more at home in your hearts, living within you as you trust in Him. May your roots go down deep into the soil of God's marvelous love.

"And may you be able to feel and understand, as all God's children should, how long, how wide, how deep, and how high His love really is; and to experience this love for yourselves (though it is so great that you will never see the end of it, or fully know or understand it). And so at last you will be filled up with God Himself.

"Now glory be to God who by His mighty power at work within us is able to do far more than we would ever dare to ask or even dream of, infinitely beyond our highest prayers, desires, thoughts, or hopes."

It was a revolution for David to become excited about God concepts. Yet even though the force of these powerful ideas was affecting him strongly, the negative force warring within would take over as he would lay down the Book or take a sip of coffee. He wanted to shove the Book aside, go to bed and forget the whole thing. In fact, he wanted to be rid of the Book. He would have liked to put it out of his frame of reference, no matter how it drew him.

Finally, he stood there with the Book in his hand, wanting to go to bed, wanting at the same time to fall flat on his face and yield to whatever sublime powers were drawing him. One of the greatest conflicts was the sensing that if he did accept all this, it would somehow gouge an irreparable hole into his relationship with Charlotte.

It was this last thought which finally gave him the determination to rid himself of this conflict, and though still torn, he carried the Book to the small incinerator in his basement.

He stood there for a full minute, pulled both ways. It had to be a permanent decision—one way or the other. He wanted it done with. Over! A set course taken and determined.

Quickly, with one motion, he pulled up the handle of the incinerator and decisively shoved the Book in. Then he quickly walked up the steps, turned off the lights and snuggled up to Charlotte in the bed.

5

The next morning David woke with a sense of normalcy, as if the warring factions within had shrunk away and he was simply David Koehler again. And for the next several weeks he spent almost every evening and weekend doing things with Charlotte, whether it was getting together with another couple for a movie, or just sitting at home watching TV and reading magazines, or having Carla Adams or someone else over for dinner.

Probably the most delightful day of all was the one spent at Clover Cliff—the area's theme amusement park, acres and acres all reminiscent of Ireland. They arrived right at opening time, went directly to the huge log flume ride where little boats were made to resemble giant shillelaghs. The two of them were assisted into one of these boats by a college-age guide, and they were whisked off along a treacherous route and finally pulled to the top of a "waterfall." From there they plummeted into the pool below, spray flying in all directions as the shillelagh front smacked the water.

They shook hands with the leprechauns and fairies walking around the grounds, ate lunch to the merry tunes of a foursome singing Irish music and dressed in green, were hauled to the top of the "sky ladder" for a tall look at the park, took a wild train ride through Leprechaun Land, and wandered through shop after shop featuring everything from four-leaf clovers to Irish hats and wall ornaments.

It was four in the afternoon by the time they left, and they headed out to their own home for the picnic they had promised themselves, all prepared and waiting in their kitchen. They hiked a short way into the hills, stopped near a small creek which had huge pine trees shielding it from the sky, and spread out their red-checked tablecloth with chicken, salads, and cake.

"Hey, you've got whiskers," Charlotte teased, feeling little-girlish and good-natured. "Come on," she kidded, popping her last bite of cake into her mouth and straightening her bright-orange sweater, "give me a whisker rub—see if it gives me red cheeks."

She came over to him and rubbed her soft cheek against his rough one. "Well," he dutifully answered, "they're the most becoming blush-red cheeks I've ever seen."

She grinned at him, disbelieving, and he stuck the four-leaf clover they had bought into her hand. "Here—*wish* yourself some red cheeks."

"Nope," she announced saucily, "more fun this way," and she put her cheek to his again.

David grinned and half sang, half spoke "their" song to her: "Everybody loves somebody some time . . . your love made it well worth waiting, for someone like you. . . ."

"Beautiful," she whispered. "You're hired. Ten dollars an hour to sing to me every night. See my husband about it—he's very generous!"

David smiled, twisted her nose, stood up and drew her to him.

There was no mention of the strain David had been under. In fact, it was several weeks before the bizarre episodes came back fully into his consciousness. It started the evening they went to see a movie with a couple from the university.

The theater was packed when they arrived; in fact, they had to stand in line for at least fifteen minutes to get tickets. It was the late show, and most of the crowd were middle-aged. But the four of them sat down about in the center of the theater where a dozen or so college students were bunched up.

The setting of the movie was China shortly before World War II, and David immediately identified strongly with the main character, a cool, alert, veteran American sailor. Perhaps the reason the film affected him so greatly was that every person the sailor loved was caught in needless tragedy, and David could feel the anguish of the man.

First there was a Chinese boy of about twenty, whom no other word but "lovable" could describe. A big grin on his face and a strong desire to please, he learned quickly from the seaman, fought his heart out for him in a fight to save a girl from prostitution, became a loyal friend. Then the Communists grabbed him just as he was trying to get back on ship, and the sailor and rest of the crew had to watch as he was tied high on a stake and cruelly tortured. Finally, as the boy screamed for someone to kill him, the main character shot him.

There was also his shipmate, who had married a lovely Chinese girl, but was not allowed off ship to visit and protect her. He swam ashore, and fearful of coming back for the medicines he needed, died there in her arms. Then his wife, though the main character tried to help her, was killed.

Later, the gunship sailed up a river to crash through a line of junks. The sailor fought well against the young Chinese manning the blockade—although he resented his captain's super-patriotism and personal pride which had led them to attack. In the fighting, a boy leader whom the sailor had met before—a boy interested only in the welfare of his country—swung at him, missed, and in self-defense the main character smashed in with a lethal thrust to his stomach.

David winced at the horror and tragedy of those terrible seconds on the screen, and sensed those around him doing the same. But beyond the group of students, there was *laughter!* David couldn't believe it—but people all over the audience were laughing at the anguish on the boy's face as he was struck in the stomach and then writhed in pain as he fell to the floor of the junk to lie there and die.

The sailor on the screen looked down, sick. The students felt it in their guts. But most of the audience was laughing, reminded of the old westerns and World War II movies of chopping down the baddies or the Japs as if it were a game, with cues to laugh as enemies toppled from the cliffs and tops of stores.

What kind of world is this where people get yuks out of

other people's anguish? David demanded of himself, glancing around. As the film rolled on and the main character himself died a senseless death, the thoughts of everyone as they walked out of the theater in near silence were serious, questioning: Why? What was the film trying to say? Patriotism is bad? Prejudice and nationalism kill? One culture cannot impose itself on another culture? But to David one thought hammered in his brain: the sheer idiocy of it, the meaningless deaths of wonderful people. Never before had he seen victims as being so human, so worthy of love, and Orientals so much more than just numbers recorded as having been starved to death or killed in bombings. How absurd that these flesh-and-blood people with personalities and smiles and loves could be killed for no real reason. Pélu's evaluations started merging with the film, and the horror of planet Earth weighed on him.

The next day he tried to put it out of his mind. However, from that point on he felt distinctly pursued, as if some force were after him, pushing him into a corner. It was one morning as he was doing research in the university library that he felt the urge to look up a poem he remembered from literature class several years ago, a poem which seemed especially to parallel his own situation. He remembered only the title—"The Hound of Heaven." He indeed felt hounded, and he wondered how this other person had made out.

He located it easily in an anthology, and read:

> I fled Him, down the nights and down the days;
>   I fled Him, down the arches of the years;
> I fled Him, down the labyrinthine ways
>   Of my own mind; and in the midst of tears
> I hid from Him, and under running laughter.
>   Up vistaed hopes I sped;
>   And shot, precipitated,
> Adown Titanic glooms of chasmed fears,
>   From those strong Feet that followed, followed after.
>   But with unhurrying chase,
>   And unperturbed pace,
> Deliberate speed, majestic instancy,
>   They beat—and a Voice beat
>   More instant than the Feet—
> "All things betray thee, who betrayest Me."

.   .   .   .

Halts by me that footfall:
Is my gloom, after all,
Shade of His hand, outstretched caressingly?
"Ah, fondest, blindest, weakest,
I am He whom thou seekest!
Thou dravest love from thee, who dravest me."

He pondered that for a long while. And then he felt compelled to go to the reference shelf and pick up the familiar design of the same contemporary edition of the Bible he had burned. He began reading the Gospel of John, which he had heard was a complete story of Jesus.

He read slowly, deliberately, sentence by sentence:

"Before anything else existed, there was Christ, with God. He has always been alive and is Himself God.

"He created everything there is—nothing exists that He didn't make.

"Eternal life is in Him, and this life gives light to all mankind. . . .

"But although He made the world, the world didn't recognize Him when He came."

David evaluated. He tried to concentrate. One force now urged him to push this aside and get some fresh air, to get the hamburger he wanted, because of a skimpy breakfast. At the same time he felt drawn to read on, to give this thing a chance.

To help him concentrate on the meaning, he pulled out his notebook and wrote down in full some of the verses:

"God did not send His Son into the world to condemn the world, but to save it.

"There is no eternal doom awaiting those who are trusting Him to save them. But those who don't trust Him have already been tried and condemned for not believing in the only Son of God.

"Their sentence is based on this fact: that the Light from heaven came into the world, but they loved their former darkness more than the Light, for their deeds were evil.

"They hated the heavenly Light because they wanted to sin in the darkness. They stayed away from that Light for fear their sins would be exposed and they would be punished."

This son of God business had always confused him. It was

absurd for him to be God himself if he was a son and therefore "begotten" or created. He'd heard professors at the university point out that he was *a* son of God, as we all are,
therefore a magnificent teacher who gave us great moral truths
as did Socrates.

Yet as he read on—through stories he'd never realized were
so *supernatural*—he wondered about these miracles and this
"Father-Son" relationship.

Who *was* this Jesus?

David started writing down statements by the man himself.

"You cannot come where I am going . . .

"You are from below; I am from above. You are from this
world; I am not . . .

"I have come to you from God . . .

"No one who obeys Me shall ever die! . . .

"The absolute truth is that I was in existence before Abraham was ever born!"

A bell rang. Students moved and replaced other students
at chairs and stools.

David read on until he read this declaration by Jesus: "I will
only reveal Myself to those who love Me and obey Me."

It was at this point that the whole issue became clear to
David. From the beginning the major question had not been
intellectual. From childhood he had realized—though he had
never consciously thought it through—that if there were even
a *chance* that such unbelievable things as the claims of this
Jesus were true, he should thoroughly investigate them and
find an answer. Too much depended on a mortal's knowing
the truth about a man who claimed to have risen from the dead
and who said he was the *only* way to happiness in the afterlife.

No, the real reason for David's reticence had always been
that force which even now made investigation distasteful. If
he were to get involved, he might lose out on some things
very pleasurable. It had always been a question of his *will*. He
didn't *want* to accept all this. He might hurt Charlotte. He had
no idea what it would mean in self-sacrifice or anything else.
All of his arguments had stemmed from this powerful force
now drawing him away from the very ideas of aligning himself
and subjecting himself to the terrible purity and rightness he
sensed here.

The conflict raged in his mind and being. He knew he wanted to reject Jesus—and probably would—because every familiar emotion and desire compelled him to. The Aelor dynamic was foreign, threatening.

Yet he wanted to accept, and with his will he cautiously pulled himself a little closer to that point of yielding, of allowing God to fill him up and shove the desires for delicious, forbidden feelings away, so that a more lasting, meaningful delight could take control. Again and again he would move toward God, but then be drawn twice as far back from him. It was as real a battle as ever he'd fought near the goal posts.

Suddenly, he dropped his head on the table and whispered in despair, "I can't. God help me. *I can't do it.* You take me!"

And in that moment, as if the one force were suddenly banished like a terrible hunger satisfied, he felt release. Full, sweet release that after his battle brought a touch of tears.

Excitement of a higher quality than he'd ever known now gripped him. He felt cleansed of all he'd been guilty of; he felt like a new person. And in a strange way, he felt lifted up —not cheated—lifted into a new life of such sweeping fullness that anything else, no matter how pleasurable or filled with power or prestige, was futile and empty.

"At God's right hand are pleasures forevermore."

Strange, but that was the phrase that kept running through David's mind—as if in answer to all the things he felt so attached to, that seemed so impossible to give up. But what kind of pleasures did God give anyway? Didn't the Bible frown on pleasures?

A myriad of such questions focused one by one in his mind. He walked over to the cafeteria for lunch, knowing that something cataclysmic had happened to him in that library. He wondered if it was "conversion." He felt elated, as if he had walked into an awesome new world and had been made a part of it. Yet at the same time he felt very "normal."

The entire next week was like that. At times he even wondered if it might not have all been in his imagination. He did little but go to work and read various translations of the Bible. Before seeking any other kind of direction in religion, he wanted to read from the original sources until he had a basis for making evaluations of any religious person's comments.

David treated the Bible like steak—he devoured it. To most, an account of his week would have been a tedious, humdrum affair. Certainly to Charlotte it was. But to David the New Testament was a revelation, and he recalled Pélu's awe at its veracity. The fresh, supernatural impact of so many of the stories and statements made him feel as if a power were flowing through him, and he took his first steps in trying to talk to God.

As he read and prayed, he had a growing sense that he had some part to play in the plans of Aelor. Hadn't Pélu himself said that this was why he'd been singled out?

And then he remembered Pélu's comment about Phelps' being a pawn of the Enemy.

Thoughts caromed off every corner of his mind as he considered the implications and at the same time the enormity and the unlikeliness of it all. Yet wasn't everything that had happened to him most unlikely? He wished very much now that he might see Pélu again.

As he was thinking along these lines, and reading in the Gospel of St. Matthew about the weaknesses of Jesus' own disciples in the face of great responsibilities, David felt fear. Though he had sensed a new joy and release since that day in the library, he also remembered his temper and undisciplined thoughts. This placement of huge responsibility on his shoulders forced the fear of inadequacy through his veins.

Here he was, a human naked of special powers—at least without the Gibraltar of Pélu, who had hinted that he might be destined to act out a drama that would affect people for eternity. He knew he was hardly up to it—that he would fail just like so many people written about in the Bible. But, too, he came to understand that *every* moral conflict is one with vast, eternal implications—a human being acting out dramas watched by millions, perhaps billions, to be etched in substance more enduring than granite. Failures or victories would touch lives for all times.

He realized he would fail. He had no doubt of this. He was too much David Koehler, the person he had always been, and as yet very little absorbed in this Aelor which dominated Pélu.

At his desk David thrust his hands over his face and whispered, "Help me. . . ."

During all this time he had tried to spend time relaxing or working around the house with Charlotte, and at times even hid the fact that he was reading the Bible. Yet she was growing increasingly apprehensive about his actions. Although he was not distraught as before, she knew he was on some "new kick," and though she did not probe, she was greatly upset and let him know it.

It came to a head one evening when she came into his den with his favorite late snack: ice cream and chocolate cake, with coffee.

"Is the bear at home?" she asked, poking her head around the corner.

He motioned her in with an expansive smile and made a place for her and the tray. For a while they talked about her classes and his day at the office. But then she picked up the book he was reading and asked, "Research for a story?"

David looked squarely into her eyes. "No—personal satisfaction. Great literature. Great truths."

"How great?" she asked. "Seems as if you've been majoring on it for some time now."

"O.K.," he said, rising and walking over to the window. "O.K., I'll give it to you straight, just exactly straight. It should be nothing at all to get upset or even unhappy about because I know you've *been* upset ever since I really started reading this thing. The simple fact is that, like a few million other Americans and humans around the world, I've come to the point in my study and research that I believe this book is accurate, that what it says is for real, that Jesus did come to save people, me included. Nothing really radical or weird about that—you can find people in any city who believe it."

"Yes, and in every asylum," Charlotte replied, watching him closely. She wanted to burn through to capture his thoughts, to see how erratic they were, to see if his brain really were going so far as to bring her world crashing down around her. "David, my question is, what does your space story have to do with it? Does it all fit together? All one ball of wax?"

"Look, Charlotte, let's not talk about the space thing. That's in the past. That's done with. *All* over. I believe the Bible— O.K. But that's no looney-bin bit. So do lots and lots of people."

"But was it this creature you supposedly talked to who got you into believing this?"

"Well, of course he influenced me."

"And next week he'll have you believing you're Napoleon. David, I don't want to be harsh or cruel, but you've *gotta* snap out of this or—"

"Or—" David cut in.

"How do I know? You get carted off somewhere or something."

"Well, what are you trying to do, threaten me? Here I am being honest with you and trying to find answers, and I've finally found one which makes sense and one which millions of other people have found too and you don't try to understand; you just want to scare me into insanity—whatever kind of therapy that is."

"Don't get violent! I'm only trying to make you see you can't keep on playing these games, because *I* certainly am not! What kind of a guy did I marry, anyway? Do you expect me to live with this for the next fifty years?"

"So I guess you'd just walk out or something, huh? Well, *don't* care about helping me, just walk out and go home to mama, or see your precious Steve Forsyth who's tossing out his woman anyway. You've got a great approach, you're standing by me all right; thanks a lot, a whole lot!"

Charlotte stood, staring coldly at her young husband, watching his eyes. "All right, maybe that's *exactly* what I need to do," she said levelly. "Maybe I'd better get out of here so I can regain *my* sanity and perspective. Look, you're convinced about this, and if you're going to go the religious route full steam ahead toot-toot-toot all-whistles-full with who knows what nutty approach it may end up with, I *will* go home till you get at least an ounce of sense in your cranium!"

"Well, go go go go go!"

Charlotte stormed out of the room, and took no more than fifteen minutes to throw some things together into her suitcase. She said good-bye—sharply—then drove off in their second car, an old black Renault.

David had always known they both had explosive tempers once they got going. But an hour later he couldn't imagine the whole thing had actually happened. His emotions even as she drove off, were boiling—he felt deeply hurt by her, even felt he had a right to lash back. But as the anger subsided, he was mixed in his desire to have her back and smooth it over, and the desire for her to realize how she had hurt him and to come back and apologize. She *had* to see the cruelty of it. . . .

But Charlotte herself was far too upset about her own future to consider anything of the sort. What she wanted most in life was security, a reasonable man, and a family where the children could grow up in a normal way. Having all this wrenched from under her did not generate feelings of pity, but panic, and a desperation to get this ironed out.

After two days, David called to apologize. He admitted he had wronged her in losing his temper. But even though Charlotte was very kind on the phone, she hedged about coming home right away. After that phone call, David wished once again he had never seen a spaceship, or for that matter a Bible either. For though this new life within him was in many ways exciting and fulfilling, the break with Charlotte was hardly bearable.

*   *   *

It was four days after the blowup that David was asked by Phelps to join him and the president of Arco to visit the person who was to become the corporation's hottest multi-million dollar property. David was highly surprised that he—or even Phelps for that matter—would be asked to go with the president, who was at least six steps above them both on the organizational chart and was a magnate not only in the recording industry but in films and radio as well. His New York City office, David had been told, was the size of a gigantic living room, and even had an imposing fireplace in it.

David was introduced to the president and two of his vice-presidents outside Phelps' office shortly before they were to visit the singer. Carlisle was the president's name. He was fifty-ish, slim, with a blotchy complexion and just wisps of hair. For some strange reason his eyes conveyed to David the feeling that he would enjoy hurting people. He shook David's hand on the introduction, but instead of making small talk, stared at him as if to analyze everything from his haircut to his brain's convolutions.

"You're the one who wrote the article on The Union Jacks?" he asked, half question, half statement.

"I did, sir."

David expected some sort of comment, but got none. Instead, the five of them were picked up by a white Lincoln Continental, then were driven through the city to a large brownstone fraternity house with wide, white shutters, all in poor repair. A dull street lamp lighted their way up the half-dozen steps, and as Phelps knocked on the door, David felt both extreme uneasiness and strong revulsion. He wondered how Phelps would bring harm to planet Earth. Were those shaggy-haired rebels against God, or were they searching for Him? Or both?

David thought of how groups had been getting dirtier and dirtier—literally—and how they were making verbal filth common. He wondered if he wanted to meet this person whom even Carlisle, on the way over, had said might be going *too* far. *How much further out* could these rebels go? David wondered.

They were admitted by a young man in tight trousers and white T-shirt, holding a can of beer in his hand. He guided them through the hall of the frat house and down the stairs to the cellar. As they continued along the musty, dark hall, David noticed a series of wine kegs à la monastery with scrawled puns such as "Keep thy head in thy hand," evidently labeling various types of alcoholic beverages. Finally, they stooped under a 2 x 6 rafter, and knocked on a splintered door covered with tiny sections of peeling paint.

"Come in."

As they walked through the doorway into the dimly lighted room, David wrinkled his nose at what he expected to confront. But rising to greet him was Clint Edwards, a star athlete at the university, his hair fashionably cropped with the All-American look, smiling amiably as he extended his hand to each of them.

6

"Walk right in," Edwards invited. He was clothed in black trousers and a blue, shaggy-hair sweater which emphasized his huge shoulders and collegiate look. The room was soft-lighted and spartan neat, with a simple desk, bed, a couple of chairs, and a good sound system with stereo speakers placed at opposite ends. The effect was quite the opposite of what David had expected.

"Yes," Carlisle was saying. "This image might do quite nicely. . . ."

Edwards was threading a tape, and at a nod from Carlisle, he turned a switch and filled the room with enormous sound. A big beat was the dominant strain to hit David's ears, yet the total effect was unique: massive, almost exhilarating, and moving over and around the almost incomprehensible lyrics. This first song increased in tempo until it broke off in a crescendo of silence. David realized then that he hadn't caught any of the words.

He listened more intently on the next, straining to catch the lyrics. At first, there was nothing but music, happy, light-hearted music which eventually blended with the words:

> Willie John, black man, sits with his Janie,
>   two little boys acrawlin' on his lap;
> Four young black folk, hold each other tight,
> It's a white, white night outside.

The tempo increased, with a sound of alarm and danger swirling around the words:

> Cold, much colder, got to get some wood.
> Willie John steps out—the whites nab him good
> No screaming, no hollerin'—they hit him
>   with a board;
> The hooded, sheeted, hellion entertainers for
>   the little town of—Elehambra.

Drums now beat, quivering, voodoo drums, and the voice no longer sang—but spoke out, almost spat out, the words:

> They got him by the creek, a hundred gathered 'round
> > They jab him,
> > burn his fingers,
> > put a noose around his neck.
> They toss him in the river,
> > They drag him out half dead . . .
> > Willie John—(the Evening's Entertainment).
> > They talk to him, they stand him up,
> > > affix the rope, and laugh . . . as
> > Willie John screams.
> (He's the Evening's Entertainment)
> and Willie John dangles
> (The Evening's Entertainment)
> > Fin'ly everyone go home, with a grisly-
> small-reminder-of
> the Evening's Entertainment.

Now the music went back to soft plaintive sounds as Edwards began singing:

> In a little shack it's still cold—
> but too white outside to get the wood
> The little-girl Janie shivers,
> > her boys shiver
> They don't know what all they got to shiver
> > about . . .
> > > 'cause Janie nineteen-year-old
> > > Janie
> > > She's a widow and she don't know yet
> She will . . . and a hundred men in white . . .

Then the last phrase—*"men still alive!"*—was ripped out with a crash of angry percussion which then took fully fifteen seconds to die away.

"What's your title on that one?" Carlisle asked.

"Either 'Men Still Alive' or 'The Evening's Entertainment.' The latter, probably."

Carlisle pursed his lips. " 'The Evening's Entertainment'—definitely."

The next song came on with a light beat. David had trouble making out the words, but it sounded like:

> Maria . . . Maria . . . Maria . . . Maria . . .
> You *must* for the sake of the family . . .

Suddenly, the music became nothing but tortured cacophony, going on and on for about fifteen seconds, and then soft sounds, more words he couldn't catch, and a change to a string solo and a girl's voice singing about a boy she's met and loves, wonderful talks and walks together, joy in the sunshine. Then the jarring noises again, and voices, and finally a girl's scream.

> Now we will all starve, Maria,
> Your knife is too bloody, Maria.

Then, a chorus of voices sang in angelic fury:

> Who killed Maria? Who killed Maria? Who
> killed Maria?

Carlisle was again the first to speak. "I didn't get it—maybe the basic gist, but that's all."

"Purposely done, of course," Edwards explained. "If you listen to it three or four times you will—and that builds up the intrigue so that when you finally do hear the whole message, it's yours and you're delighted with yourself because a lot of others—including most adults—haven't bothered to get those words."

"So tell us," Carlisle demanded. "We can't strain on every word a half-dozen times tonight."

"Maria," Edwards explained, "is made to live as a mistress with a rich old man because her family is starving. She hates his touch, but can't stand to see her family starve, so she submits. Then she meets the handsome son, grows to love him, talks to him, he likes her. But then comes the heartwrenching scene when her lover finds out about her and his father. He despises her for what she has to do—and tells her so in vilifying terms. So, Maria kills herself."

"And," Carlisle asked, "who *did* kill Maria—the old man, the family, the boy? Any or all of 'em, huh?" he grunted.

Edwards smiled. "Whatever the listener thinks . . . society in general, of course."

He then flicked the switch for the next song, a militant, crusading kind of thing called "The Relics." It was a challenge to face the future without "the relics of the past" which muddied lives, built prejudices, forced people into artificial molds, choked love between boy and girl . . . *"to rise to all that is noble in the human breast, to crush injustice and make the world a garden instead of a garbage pit."*

Carlisle was sitting on one of the chairs, drumming his fingers on the arm. "Just wish the whole approach were a trifle more subtle," he said, almost to himself. "There's always that thin line between attacking the Establishment and sounding like part of it—wanting to 'cure injustice.' "

Phelps commented, "I think the kids are just *waiting* for this kind of thing. It's right on, with the gut issues, and—"

"But Clint doesn't look like a rebel," Carlisle explained. "I'm not saying it's a problem. But he *could* be labeled *Establishment* if it isn't handled just right. A little more subtlety, yet still all the fire, indignation, demand for a new world."

As David listened to the conversation, he was surprised. Carlisle had distinctly impressed him somehow as intrinsically evil, yet here he was pushing this approach. David had walked in thinking that if this were in any way orchestrated by the Twisted One, it would be slime, oozing and choking what morality and integrity remained. Yet David himself was profoundly moved and challenged as he listened to the anguished cries against injustice, the pleas to rise to the nobility in man.

"Did you read that mock-epic story of the pop singer who challenged his 'troops' to campaign for the vote for fourteen-year-olds?" Phelps was asking David. "Nobody thought them serious until he put 4,000,000 demonstrating kids into Sunset Strip. Pretty soon the whole country allowed all teen-agers to vote. Then they elected their singing idol as President, teen-agers ran everything, adults were put into concentration camps."

Phelps lighted a cigarette and flipped the match neatly into a nearby waste can. "That's not the kind of takeover we'll see, obviously. But winning the hearts and minds of youth and putting them in the right direction, giving them goals, stamping out injustice—that is the only thing that will save our country —and maybe the whole world—from mass chaos or anarchy or who knows what?"

Carlisle was ignoring Phelps' conversation with Clint Edwards, and soon he was walking toward the door. Phelps cut short his comments and quickly followed ... and within fifteen minutes they were back at the office. As David was getting out, Carlisle looked at him, his face expressionless, but his eyes alive with suction, and said abruptly, "Phelps here told me you act very strangely when it comes to talk about UFO reports. What's the story?"

David flushed, and he could tell Carlisle sensed he had something. But he simply replied, "Oh, just an interest of mine, sir."

Carlisle eyed him awhile longer, then motioned for the driver to take off.

*　　*　　*

For the next few days, the thing uppermost in David's mind was his loneliness without Charlotte. The entire house reminded him of her, every object, every meal. He wanted so much to call her, yet he didn't want to be premature and make the situation worse.

At the same time, however, he was fascinated by the part he might have to play in some plan of Aelor's. Why else had he been chosen to board a space craft, to hear all this? Yet he couldn't imagine what his part might be. He sensed that somehow it would be tied to Arco, yet how?

The only possible source of information he had was the Bible itself, so he pored over its pages and tried to relate it to his own experiences. Several verses helped him understand some of Pélu's comments. For instance, Colossians 1:16: "And Christ Himself is the Creator who made everything in heaven and earth, the things we can see and the things we can't; the spirit world with its kings and kingdoms, its rulers and authorities: all were made by Christ for His own use and glory."

David wished that the passage had gone into much greater detail. Were spirits simply human-type creatures in another plane—millions of them, with echelons of power and wealth? Were they possibly right here on earth, not visible, but in another dimension? How many might there be?

He was just as interested in a passage in the tenth chapter

of Daniel in which the writer was met by "a person robed in linen garments, with a belt of purest gold around his waist and glowing, lustrous skin. From his face came blinding flashes like lightning, and his eyes were pools of fire; his arms and feet shone like polished brass, and his voice was like the roaring of a vast multitude."

David did not feel the description fit Pélu. Daniel's visitor understood evil and its result, as Pélu did not. Yet David strongly identified with Daniel as he read the story from the Old Testament:

"And I heard his voice—'Oh Daniel, greatly beloved of God,' he said, 'stand up and listen carefully to what I have to say to you, for God has sent me to you.' So I stood up, still trembling with fear.

"Then he said, 'Don't be frightened, Daniel, for your request has been heard in heaven and was answered the very first day you began to fast before the Lord and pray for understanding; that very day I was sent here to meet you.

" 'But for twenty-one days the mighty Evil Spirit who overrules the kingdom of Persia blocked my way. Then Michael, one of the top officers of the heavenly army, came to help me, so that I was able to break through these spirit rulers of Persia.

" 'Now I am here to tell you what will happen to your people, the Jews, at the end times—for the fulfillment of this prophecy is many years away.'

"All this time I was looking down, unable to speak a word.

"Then someone—he looked like a man—touched my lips and I could talk again; and I said to the messenger from heaven, 'Sir, I am terrified by your appearance and have no strength.

" 'How can such a person as I even talk to you? For my strength is gone and I can hardly breathe.'

"Then the one who seemed to be a man touched me again, and I felt my strength returning.

" 'God loves you very much,' he said; 'don't be afraid! Calm yourself; be strong—yes, strong!' Suddenly as he spoke these words, I felt stronger and said to him, 'Now you can go ahead and speak, sir, for you have strengthened me.'

"He replied, 'Do you know why I have come? I am here

to tell you what is written in the Book of the Future. Then, when I leave, I will go again to fight my way back, past the prince of Persia; and after him, the prince of Greece. Only Michael, the angel who guards your people Israel, will be there to help me.' "

So this creature Daniel saw must have been created higher than man, higher than Pélu. Did he simply take the form of a person to appear to Daniel? Or was that his true form?

And what of this "Twisted One"? David had always thought the Bible said *God* ruled earth. Yet, it also spoke of Satan as the ruler of this world. Was planet Earth exclusively Satan's? He remembered from the Book of Job that Satan had to get permission to torment that good man. Possibly Satan had full power within limits, or perhaps on everyone but people linked to Aelor.

David was fascinated by the implications of all this. Did it mean every human was unwittingly under Satan's power, unless he were controlled by Christ? Yet what of self-sacrificing non-Christians who opened orphanages, fought disease, gave of themselves to die for others? What of all the secular progress and development on earth?

Of course, if Satan had been cast down to earth because he wanted to be bigger than God and "exalt his throne above the stars of God," maybe Satan didn't want his one and only domain to be shambles. After all, he had his pride! Building a great technology and well-ordered system—with occasional violence to produce despair and hatreds—would be better than making earth a total hell from which people would cry out to God. And maybe pride in good people—the pride of erecting a hospital or church—at times was akin to Satan's own fall. On the other hand, man had originally been "made in the image of God." Was genuine compassion a vestige of that?

David's intense interest in the Bible and his conviction that he was living in a flow of power identical to that which Pélu experienced drove him more and more to want to share this with others. It seemed absurd to him that he had gone all his life completely oblivious to this dynamic which was now changing his life. It was inconceivable that anyone, if clearly faced with these facts, would reject them.

It was this train of thought which led to the idea now burning in his mind as the most exciting thing since he had first seen Pélu's ship.

He had learned in a college course that walls and other solid objects retain all sounds—including words—which have resounded against them. His professor had said, "All science must do is perfect a way to unscramble these sounds and play them back, and we'll have a complete tape-recorded history —word for word!"

What if Jesus' exact words, in His voice, could be played to the world!

The thought tantalized him. If Pélu were so advanced scientifically, he could solve something like this. And if David had some task to do, might it not be to find out if the Bible *were* accurate . . . if Christ *did* make all those statements . . . if Christ *did* rise from the dead? If proven, the entire planet— half the souls that had ever lived now living, more than three billion of them—could be snatched from the Enemy.

But he would have to have Pélu.

At first that did not seem to be such an obstacle—time after time the humanoid had forced himself upon him. Surely he would be happy to help in such a thing.

Yet, as the days passed, David realized that this was illogical thinking. He had no way to contact Pélu, and he had told him to get out of his life. Being the creature of integrity that he was, Pélu had probably honored the request.

The thing which most allowed Giant Despair to climb aboard his shoulders and pummel him toward the ground, however, was the fact that when he called Charlotte again, she had still been hesitant about coming home. It was Steve Forsyth that worried him. A student at the university had mentioned seeing Forsyth's car at Charlotte's mother's home.

Six days after the Carlisle meeting, David was sitting in his den one evening reading Tolkien's trilogy when in the frame of the doorway appeared a big muscular figure, made even larger by the smallness of the door frame. The light reflected from his face flickered burnished bronze.

"Pélu!"

It was the first time David had ever shown joy on meeting him. This time he leaped at the humanoid like an old college buddy, grasped his hand, then led him to the sofa.

Pélu was grinning. "So, now we are brothers, in a thousand ways. And you have a plan within the will of Aelor. It is good. I have been reading your thoughts at times, you know."

The exhilaration David felt at that moment could have been enhanced only by Charlotte's walking in and completing the trio . . . which thought immediately reminded him of his most pressing problem.

"Pélu—you *must* stay here till Charlotte can meet you. You simply *have* to!"

"Of course," he quickly agreed. "I've been planning on precisely that. I hadn't realized your predicament. But first let's talk about your plan."

"You think it's feasible?"

"Oh, of course," Pélu replied, pulling out his pocket computer. "In fact, with sufficient earth data, it could be handled by this small unit—with enough time. But we'll use a larger one from the ship . . . I'm afraid earth computers are not sufficiently miniaturized to do the job even if we could program one."

They discussed procedures at great length that evening and agreed that their greatest job was not to set up the program but to put it into the hands of the right scientists who could honestly and effectively procure and process the data—and have the reputation to insure acceptance by the world. As they talked, David typed out an agreement binding the scientists to exploration of the still-intact judgment hall of Pilate, the crucifixion site, the resurrection area, etc. The project would be aimed at the authentication of the words of Jesus Christ and the activities of Biblical account. Hopefully, an open report verified by eight methods and by various observers could be released by Christmas.

Pélu stayed with David that night. Next morning, he summoned the spacecraft and they carried out an eighty pound computer which Pélu pointed out could not only develop the project on Jesus' words, but was capable of coordinating all the activities—every individual's detailed work pattern—on earth. It also had enough knowledge stored to revolutionize the planet technologically. They placed it in David's den.

"Nine o'clock. I'd better call Charlotte," David suggested.

He reached her at her mother's, and she was warm as usual,

but firm. "What are you trying to tell me, David? Sure, maybe I should be there. But how do I know that's best?"

David was optimistic now—if necessary he'd drive over there *with* Pélu. "O.K.," he said, trying to sound as cool as possible. "Look, I won't even ask you to come and stay. How about just a date? Come over here for dinner tomorrow night. I've gotten really good on char-broiled steak, and I'll have you back at mother's by 10:30—I promise."

David was almost surprised at how quickly she agreed to that, and he told her he'd pick her up at five.

After chatting for a while, Pélu suggested that they board the craft and leave, then come back in time for their meeting with Charlotte. "I do not want the craft here all day. And we have much to discuss. We should talk at length about Arco and this singer Edwards. Can you bring along your tapes of his music?"

David did have them, and as he followed Pélu to the spacecraft, he carried them in a small leather case. While crossing the field behind his house, David thought he noticed Phelps' green convertible parked quite some distance away. He couldn't be sure, but if it weren't his, it had to be an identical model. If Phelps were around. . . .

7

A device like a ladder, but with just one rung, descended from the outside edge of the ship which was elevated above the belly resting on the ground. Pélu put his foot on the rung, and when he applied his weight, it began lifting him up. Another soon moved into its place, and David rode that one up. Soon they were in the magnificent craft, and they gazed through portholes in the control room as the craft effortlessly, soundlessly lifted up and sped into the clouds. Several times they saw planes in one direction or another, and Pélu neatly avoided them by touching small knobs on the huge console under a series of three large portholes. There were no seats here; they stood as they traveled.

Once a military plane started chasing them. Pélu accelerated, and still it came on. Finally, Pélu gave the knob a full half twist, and the plane blinked out of sight.

Within minutes they were fluttering down, engines off, and hit the water, then sank. To David it was like re-living an unbelievable dream.

Long before they hit bottom, Pélu walked away from the controls and guided David into his beautiful living room with its warm and colorful diffused lighting. Exotic, commanding music flooded the room, music of a dynamic nature, like cascading water or roaring jets, accompanied by strange visual representations of scenic wonder in 3-D throughout the room, with wildlife all totally foreign to David.

At times, as they sat talking, he would notice among the brilliantly colored scenes creatures or mountains which were colorless. Yet on his comment to Pélu about this, he got just a quizzical stare. Dogs and other animals on earth, David had read, can see colors humans are not equipped to see. Apparently, here were colors before his eyes, but like a color TV program on a black-and-white screen, it came through dull and drab.

Yet David could not have described the pleasantness of the overall effect of the scenes and music—though they were meant strictly as background as the two men talked.

"I'm excited, with you," Pélu was saying, "about this reconstruction of Christ's words. Your planet should be revolutionized, the Enemy thwarted in his plans to steal those meant for joy. He will be sent to his own torment."

"His own torment?" David asked.

"I have been digesting your book from Aelor. It says that the Twisted One will end up in the place reserved for him and his mighty host. Apparently, it was never meant for anyone but him and his. But many humans go there, too, because they live for the enemy, not Aelor."

David sat in the chair, his attention diverted by the idyllic flame-red mountain scenes, and creatures like giant kittens—

bright canary yellow—gamboling under a waterfall of very dense, bright-green liquid.

"Where do you think that place of torment is?" David asked. "The next dimension? This dimension? Will there be some terrible explosion and everything made over?"

Pélu smiled and touched the surface of the table in front of them. Immediately the entire top spun upside down and became one huge piece of paper, with precise square marking tools affixed as if by magnets. "I have no more facts than you, David. But I can make hypotheses. And while I'm doing it, I'll explain a little of what we know about matter and space so you'll be oriented to my thinking."

Pélu scratched out a simple map and shoved it toward David, who looked at it in fascination.

"You see, everything visible to your telescopes is part of the dead sphere of antimatter. It is no longer growing and expanding like the rest of the universe. It is void, lifeless. The quasars, as I told you before, are the violent meeting of matter and antimatter. No being or thing can pass from one to the other without exploding with more force than a sun. Antimatter is all the Enemy's domain."

Pélu looked over at David. "I read in a book of yours that one of the many theories on the universe is that it's one mass explosion, all moving with force from some unknown center. This is true. The center of explosion is the center of the universe *in this dimension*. Beyond it in all directions is infinity— an always growing, ever-expanding infinity, so that no matter how fast you traveled you could never come to the end of it. There is no end.

"Everything outside antimatter—that is, everything in matter—is ruled by the creatures of Aelor. We are privileged to share in his creativity by filling it with living beings and taming the uncharted regions—and in our ever-expanding universe, never will we come to an end of finding new worlds to conquer, new worlds to fill with people linked to Aelor and ruled by beings made by him.

"On the other hand, it seems to me that the Enemy and all those who follow him are, by their very nature, so corrupted that they eventually will not want the company of any other. Their selfishnesses drive them apart, for they are only good to one another as objects of exploitation. If one has no power over the other, he'll seek aloneness, and all the lusts and appetites they have will go unassuaged in their loneliness.

"If there are one hundred billion stars—or 'suns'—in antimatter, this means there will be more than enough celestial bodies for each damned being to have his own private hell."

David looked at him sharply. "You mean each one in a flaming sun thousands of degrees? Hell can't be *that* literal, can it?"

"Oh," Pélu said, "I have no idea. There would be planets around many of the suns, of course, Who knows—I'm simply pointing out that there's plenty of room in antimatter. Maybe, on the other hand, hell will be a small, compact place where evil spirits can taunt and torment each other, whether physically or mentally or emotionally or both.

"Now," he continued, "picture yourself on a staircase, which reaches to infinity both up and down. Each step represents a dimension. When we 'die,' it is like moving to another step, another dimension. Each contains totally different worlds and creatures we can visit at Aelor's pleasure. And, of course, anything that is his pleasure becomes pleasure for us, for we really are part of him."

"But is the curse of antimatter in all dimensions?" David asked, incredulous at the concepts.

"I don't know. The Enemy, of course, can go into only two. And consider this: antimatter is constantly in a state of falling in upon itself. It will never, except for some cataclysm, seem smaller to those in it, but just as within a pinhead you can have billions of worlds—molecules, atoms, protons—so in matter is antimatter a tiny bubble becoming tinier and tinier. Eventually, I suppose, a person could swallow it without noticing. It will remain as large and hideous as ever here, but will be totally lost in Aelor's dimensions."

"How do you know all this?" David asked.

"I don't," the humanoid admitted. "That is, some of it I don't. Reading your Bible and seeing the plans Aelor has, this is what I have surmised . . . .

"But one thing I *do* know. My analysis of antimatter shows that the fulfillment of Jesus' comment—the stability of the very heavens will be broken up—will not be far in the future.

Also, as your books state, the astronomic and microscopic have the same relative distance between bodies—so infinity extends in largeness and smallness of mass as well—all *quite* beyond our comprehension."

They walked over to the charting section near the controls and Pélu started explaining the geography of antimatter in more detail, letting David handle the intricate but fascinating equipment which lighted and rotated a huge, lighted map.

"There," Pélu said, "bring earth back into focus. Now, where would my home be from here?"

David struggled with the three knobs he had seen shown, then indicated a direction.

"Right! Now all you have to do is go as fast as the speed of light and in twenty-five billion years you'll be there. Think you'll be around that long?" He smiled, then led David back to the living room. Pélu picked up David's small recorder and placed the tape on it.

"You adjust this while I figure a way to energize it. We don't use plugs the way you do."

David felt right at home—strangely—and adjusted the tape for the first song. Pélu came back, and having done nothing David could see about the electricity, simply turned it on and it operated perfectly.

The music was a harsh contrast to what had been playing a few moments before, a contrast like that of pain to pleasure —sharp, jagged, yet in its own way of value—as stinging Merthiolate sometimes is.

They sat listening, and Pélu concentrated. After playing it through twice, the bronze man rose and walked to the porthole, staring into the black, murky deep. Suddenly he flicked a light, watched as a few frightened forms of marine life swam away, then turned it off.

"I knew there was something in the Enemy's plan with this music," he announced. "How it will fit, I don't know. But, even though there is much truth in the songs and humans need to be jolted, this is a terrible weapon they are forging."

David admitted his perplexity and his frank appreciation for what the music was trying to say.

"Analyze it," Pélu demanded. "As you listen to the song about the Negro, what do you feel?"

David paused, introspecting, digging. "Several things. Outrage against injustice . . . and," he finally admitted, "hatred against the whites."

"Yes, hatred," Pélu said. "You humans would respond in just that way. Earth needs more outrage against injustice. But hatred spiced with acting on a just cause is a fine tool in the hand of the Enemy. And the song of the girl who killed herself?"

"Anger," David responded. "Just sheer anger."

"Yes, but against whom?"

"The old man. The family. And the young guy." Then David paused a bit. "Maybe against God a bit, too, for allowing such a thing as poverty to cause it."

"You're developing some very useful emotions for the enemy," Pélu pointed out. "You see, Jesus, when he was on earth, became angry with injustices. He drove out the merchants with whips. But you humans allow hatred to replace anger, to eat inside you and tear you apart; you want to hurt someone, not simply stop bad things from happening. That verse, 'Vengeance is mine; I will repay, saith the Lord,' is not just an idea. It's a fact of your world. You are so much a part of evil that for you to exact revenge would necessitate your executing yourself."

David was starting to feel defensive again, and Pélu sensed it. "Sorry," he said. "Just explaining the basic problem. Now 'The Relics.' That's the most obvious. What are they lashing out against? The old rules—like the Ten Commandments? Discard morality and be new men. And most important— appeal to 'what is noble in man'! *Nothing is*—and excuse me for saying it—except for what comes from Aelor. So they're stirring you up to change your world by all the goodness in you—like labeling some men bad and killing them."

David sat there, digesting all this. He wasn't sure he quite understood all this thinking—nor agreed with it. "Do you mean these lyrics will cause violence in the streets, teen-age vigilantes redressing each maddening injustice?"

Pélu smiled good naturedly. "I've been here such a short time and never knew of evil before. Yet I think I comprehend your Prince of the Air—Satan—better than you who obeyed him and his agents for so many years. I doubt that he *always* wants violence. But he seems to have the concept implanted in many that the answer to injustice is killing. Of course, you notice how Christ met injustice done to *him*. He *loved* his enemies. He hated injustice and lashed out against it—as we should. But it's love that's the essential opposite of our enemy's plan. Thus Jesus even allowed himself to be crucified."

At that instant, a loud sound came from the control room, and both David and Pélu rose to their feet. David looked to his host, who started walking in great, swift strides to the scene of the noise, at the same time flicking a switch which instantly flooded the entire craft with bright lights.

As they reached the control room, they saw nothing awry. But Pélu slid back a panel.

There, in the adjoining room, cowered two men. One of them was Phelps, the other the fat man with the camera. Phelps, though obviously frightened, was pointing what David surmised was a .45 automatic.

"Gentlemen," Pélu said sternly. "You were not invited aboard this craft. But you will certainly not be hurt and you have no reason for fear. Why do you point that weapon at us?"

David wondered how they had gotten on the craft. The only thing he could think of was the clue of Phelps' car. Apparently they had boarded when he and Pélu were in the house.

"We're taking you back," Phelps announced. "Whether you're dead or alive is up to you. But this is one UFO that's going to be investigated—and we'll have the pilot to question as well."

"I'm sorry," Pélu replied, "but that would be quite impossible. It would not be the will of Aelor. And you could not fly this craft without me." The bronze, muscled being stared with flashing, piercing eyes at the men.

Suddenly Phelps was yelling, "No! No! You *won't* control my mind! No!"

Pélu had already taken several steps toward the men, but then stopped.

Phelps regained his composure, the gun still wavering in Pélu's direction. "Now take this vehicle back to dry land, or I'll kill you," he said, biting off his words.

The bronze man refused to move.

Phelps stood there glaring at the man, appraising the situation. He demanded again that Pélu fly the craft back. Pélu did not move or answer. Phelps renewed his demand again and again, getting more emotional and determined each moment, as if possessed by a strange force. "You won't be harmed, you fool. We just want to see what makes this ship run! Now fly it! Don't you know what this thing can do?" he asked, glancing at the ugly, squarish black object in his hand.

"I know. But I cannot fly this ship back and give you control. It would not be the will of Aelor."

"You *will!*" Phelps threatened. He pointed directly at Pélu's shoulder and commanded, "Move to the controls, or so help me I'll blow your arm off!"

"Phelps!" David yelled, seeing the craze in his eyes. "You wretched idiot!"

"Shut up!" Phelps aimed the gun carefully. "Move!" he commanded. "Move!"

Pélu simply stood there. The livid earthling pulled the trigger, and a chunk of steel splattered into the bronze man's shoulder, spinning him around and ripping open a wide, ugly hole.

"Now! See what you forced me to do!" Phelps was ranting. "Move! Get this thing out of the water!"

David started to move toward the wounded man, but Phelps angrily motioned him away by pointing the automatic at him.

Pélu was again facing the man with the gun, staring impassively at the smaller man whose fear was obviously mixed with the anger on his face. Again and again he repeated his demands for the space visitor to move, but Pélu simply glared at him, his hand clutching the ragged shoulder wound, blood trickling over his fingers. "I told you. It is not the will of Aelor. But I will put you safe on the ground."

"Who is this Aelor? And why aren't you afraid?" Phelps demanded. "*Why!* Don't you people die? You must! You bleed. Another bullet, and no more blood. No more life."

"I would move to the next world, yes," Pélu agreed. "But Aelor is there. Why should I fear?"

They stared at each other. "You're dying now," Phelps pointed out. "Drop by drop, unless you get help. We'll take you to a hospital. Move this thing!"

"Not under your command," Pélu insisted. "Give me that

weapon." Obviously Phelps was too terrified or determined or both to comply. "Don't you care at all that you die!" he fairly screamed. "Don't you have anyone who would want you back from this trip!"

At that, David noticed a strange response in Pélu's eyes. His wife. His offspring at home. Suddenly there *was* an inner conflict, and David could almost feel the struggle grow into his own chest. To obey Aelor and leave his family for another world separated from them, or possibly . . . possibly . . .

Pélu stared, the muscles in his face twitching, obviously fighting something within—confronting for the first time in centuries the great temptation of a free moral agent to choose.

Phelps, too, noticed the change and quickly followed with, "How do you *know* about the next world? Maybe it doesn't exist. Maybe *you'll* cease to exist. Maybe this Aelor isn't real. Or maybe you'll be thrown into a hell—"

At that moment David screamed at Phelps, throwing himself behind the safety of the sliding walls partially open. At that, Pélu lunged at Phelps, and caught the full explosion of the gun in his chest even as he was in mid-air. It smashed his chest open and at the same time slammed him to the side.

David thought Pélu must have been instantly killed, but he wrenched himself up and grabbed a lever with his right arm, then yanked all the way down.

The craft was suddenly, violently thrust straight up through the water, and the G forces flattened everyone. David lost consciousness, quickly awakened and tried to crawl toward Pélu, but couldn't even move an arm.

They were already high into the air and the G forces were now abating. The men were advancing on Pélu, and as the terribly wounded man watched, Phelps aimed the .45 at him.

This time Pélu, from his knees, yanked on the console with what must have been preternatural strength, his life's blood now spreading across the floor, and upset a whole array of equipment so that the bullet intended for him smashed into tons of metal instead.

David knew Phelps didn't think him a threat. He started to sneak behind him so he could knock the gun from his hands. He had already detached a rod from the porthole to use as a weapon.

But Pélu had dragged himself around the other way, coming up behind the two men. They spotted him as he was reaching for another switch. Phelps fired again, but hit only the flesh in his lower arm. It gave Pélu the time he needed to leap forward and grab them both. At the same instant two walls snapped shut, blocking David from them. Apparently Pélu had meant to lock them in, but had locked David out instead.

David stood pounding on the thick transparent wall, at the same time fumbling for something to open it. If the bronze man had been an earthling he would surely be dead by now. With ebbing strength he fought with Phelps for the gun while using his feet to disable the other man. In a final, wrenching twist, he tried to pull the gun into his own hands, but dropped back and crumpled onto the floor, motionless.

Phelps, shaking, gripped the gun with both of his bloody, slippery hands, and put a bullet through the back of the lifeless man's head.

David screamed in rage and frantically looked for the controls. Along the side of the compartment he saw a wide, metal bar which could obviously be pulled down. He thought he knew what it was. The men were in the same compartment he had originally entered—the one with a trap door. He jerked the bar down and as abruptly as his action, there was no floor under the men in the compartment.

Both earthlings screamed as the violent blast ripped in, tearing Pélu out of the compartment. Phelps' companion was instantly slammed against the sheer wall of the room, and clutching wildly at it, was scooped out.

Only Phelps had a chance. His fingers had clutched a metal rod half way from the ceiling along one wall. The bottom of his torso hung out and was viciously chewed at by the wind, while his whitened knuckles holding him from death weakened and weakened as his involuntary screams rose in intensity.

David gazed at this sight with satisfaction. The surge of feelings which made him activate that trap door were now fed by the sight of that murderer hanging above his death. Yet he eased the metal bar back up. The floor came half way across the room, striking Phelps in the stomach, and barely giving him time to pull himself up onto it before he could be crushed between the wall and the sliding floor.

Phelps lay there in agony. David walked away from the scene, threw himself on the couch and beat at the soft material with his fists. He did not weep. He simply allowed his hot emotions to surge through him, moment after moment. Then he walked to the control panel to ascertain the damage and figure how to land the craft.

Some of the machinery was broken, and the controls would not respond to his touch. Somehow, they were locked into place. He pushed and pulled, poked and searched for buttons. But nothing happened. In frustration he looked toward a porthole.

Below in the blackness of space, precisely like an astronaut's full-color photo, hung planet earth, a huge, round ball, with familiar continental shapes.

In terror David searched around the control room, knowing he *had* to do something to reverse the craft's direction. He pushed all the buttons and pulled every lever he could find, working frantically.

But eventually he knew he was beaten. And by the time he turned to the porthole again, no planet was visible. Everything looked like distant stars on a clear evening, only far brighter.

The hopelessness of it crushed in on him. He reacted with bitter frustration. His thoughts of Phelps—and of Phelps' being in his power—were the only things which seemed sweet or meaningful to him now.

He walked over to the transparent wall and stared at the wretched man who was now sitting in a corner. Upon seeing David, Phelps sprang to the wall and exclaimed, "Koehler! Where have you been? Get me out of this room! We've got to get this thing down! We're beyond earth, man. Do you realize? *Do you realize!*" he demanded, gesticulating wildly at the porthole.

David made no sign of recognition. He simply stared at the man, then turned his back and walked away.

He found the control console to the "laboratory" in which Phelps was trapped. There was no coding on the switches, buttons, and levers, so he methodically began trying each one.

Some controls merely raised or lowered the ceiling or floor or put in tables and lamps. Others introduced various tools, from writing instruments to flexible hands. David manipulated them around the terrified Phelps. With one switch, the entire room poured down a soapy substance and water, drenching the man, much to David's amusement.

He finally located the set he was looking for. The steel arms projected out at Phelps and finally pinned him against the wall. Then David eased out the scalpel and manipulated it slowly, ever so slowly up to the throat of the man.

"Koehler! Koehler!" he was screaming.

David started the knife down deliberately, allowing a new force to control him. He wasn't sure he wanted to kill Phelps, but if the knife were a bit clumsy, he wouldn't care about that. The knife sliced through the skin in a few places. Blood oozed. He stripped the man of his clothes, set the room temperature down, and walked back to the living room.

Turmoil controlled him, and he couldn't relax, but paced back and forth from porthole to porthole, trying to see something. Stars were abundant, but it was like having a moonless night sky in all directions, with no frame of reference, certainly no friendly earth on which to gaze. Inside himself he felt a growing sense of bitterness toward Phelps, almost as if a sadistic demon had come aboard in Phelps and had now taken over David.

He retraced his steps to the charting section and the maps. This area was undamaged; the viewer still focused on earth. After working the knobs David ascertained that they were still less than a light year away. *Going the speed of light, it'll take only twenty-five billion years to get to Pélu's planet,* he thought humorlessly. *Maybe faster we could make it in twenty . . . how about ten? Or maybe even just five billion years. Now that's not so long. I could live to be a hundred . . . years,* he muttered darkly.

He went back to Phelps' compartment and stared at the man. He glared back. Finally David walked away, and took the time to use the metal arm to shove his clothes back to him, such as they were after the cutting.

After this, David continually sought ways to gain control of the ship. He had the necessary navigation equipment. If he could simply change the course or somehow get to the source of power. . . . But everything was perfectly sealed up, and he had no tools of any kind to pry with.

(92)

Each hour, each day, was like the last. Outside, blackness with bright stars in every direction. Inside, a thousand pleasant sights and sounds to choose from, and much food. However, he could not read the "books," for they were tiny electronic tubes used for brain-wave "reading."

These were pleasant surroundings, but terribly unpleasant feelings roared through him and a thousand concerns about Charlotte plagued him.

Finally, on the eighth day, he walked over to Phelps and said with deep sarcasm, "Well, they probably have something special prepared for *you*."

Phelps rose and came up against the glass. "What do you mean?" he asked, weariness in his voice, well aware of the despairing look on David's face.

"Demons, of course. You've read all the classics about them. You know—you become theirs to feed upon. Your terror and anguish becomes their pleasure. They probably won't roast you over spits, but I imagine they have more sophisticated means to torment you. You might even have your own private cauldron to writhe in—there are a hundred billion suns, you know—more than enough for each murderer. Of course, demons probably like to slither together to enjoy their feasts."

"You're mad!" Phelps exclaimed. "You're mad, and you're driving me to the same thing. Look, you fool, the only thing we have to fear is that creature's own people, and this space ship is probably aimed there right now. They'll know we killed him and—"

"Correction," David said. "*You* killed him. I was his friend, remember? But don't worry. I figure it will take us about twenty-five billion years to get there. Until then, you're all mine!"

David knew he was speaking inanely, but felt the terrible sensation of enjoying the tormenting of Pélu's murderer. And each time he remembered that word murderer, he found ample excuse to torment.

The twenty-five billion years was a lie. As Pélu had told him, the craft was capable of consistently doubling its speed. Apparently this was what was happening, and eventually David calculated that they had traveled a full five billion light years from earth. The earth's sun was increasingly difficult to keep in sight on the viewer, even with the sophisticated multiple fix equipment. Bright stars appeared in great diversity, and instead of being simply white, each changed color from bluish to reddish glow as the spacecraft flashed past. And, directly ahead of him, at about the same distance as earth was behind, was an increasing brilliance. Eventually it began to nearly blind him as he stared at it.

Twice, a flash of great brightness and heat seemed to swallow up the spacecraft for the slightest instant, and then be gone. He wondered if possibly their speed was now so great they could pass through solid and gaseous bodies without affecting the craft or the body.

Then, as he was keeping earth's star—the sun—clearly in view one evening, it happened. Like a flickering bulb, dying, it simply fizzled out. Then blackness. Nothing he did on the equipment would bring it back. He calculated the distance away at that point to be roughly seven billion light years.

Had the solar system begun then? Had he outraced its earliest light? Had he watched its birth like a film running backwards?

They were now quickly approaching the brilliance before them. Dread haunted David as he recalled Pélu's words that at the quasars began matter, and that David's body would become a super H-bomb as soon as it came into contact with it.

The fear intensified as they approached the quasars and the heat increased. The brilliance became too terrible to look at through the portholes or on the charting equipment. In desperation, he went to Phelps.

"Listen," he said to the filthy, unshaven man, "we're about to explode! We've got to get this thing turned around somehow!"

"You idiot, that's what I've been saying for weeks!"

David, holding a piece of pipe in his hand for protection, slid the walls back. Phelps ran immediately to the control area. Throughout the trip, his fevered brain must have been focused on getting to it, for he pushed, wrenched, shoved, twisted. But no response.

The heat was rapidly becoming unbearable, and the two worked frantically on finding a solution. The entire interior of the craft was bathed with a light so painfully brilliant that they shut their eyes to work by touch. David glanced quickly at the viewer. The millions of stars surrounding them all seemed to be collapsing into a central point before them.

They were screaming at each other to hurry when the ship rocked violently and suddenly there was a cataclysmic explosion which deafened the two men and threw them into unconsciousness.

8

David came back to consciousness very slowly, as if his lungs and throat and head were all emptying themselves of a murky, heavy blackness. He was sprawled flat on his stomach, his legs pinned under some painful weight.

Wherever he was, it was black except for intermittent flashes of blue light. He turned his head to the right and saw dimly, not five inches away from his right elbow, the smashed corner of some huge machinery which had overturned and now was balanced, he thought, quite precariously against the wall. As David stared into the blackness, the flashes of blue light illuminated the floor enough to reveal a hand—obviously Phelps'—motionless, pinned beneath some wreckage.

David simply lay there, as if in the middle of the night after a strange dream, trying to piece things together. It was inconceivable that he had survived the violence of that explosion. Their direct course into the quasars, if Pélu had been right, meant they should be bits of molecules now.

Maybe they hadn't survived, David thought, suddenly appalled. After all, what was death? There had to be some waking up like this, didn't there?

His mind raced. Could it be that death—the instant his and Phelps' lives were ended by the explosion—simply transported them into another dimension, identical to the first, including the spacecraft? The same suns, the same planets, the same vast stretches of space, with living souls going from one dimension to another?

Or had they simply crashed before really hitting the quasars, to be trapped now in the emptiness of antimatter on some barren planet?

David tested his legs, slowly trying to pull them free. A painful fact quickly flashed to his brain—one leg was broken or crushed.

After some moments of simply lying there, he twisted around and spent at least fifteen minutes inching and pulling his good leg free. Then, bracing his foot against the wall, he was able to shove away the metal debris and free himself.

He grasped the corner of a bent lighting device and pulled himself up. David saw that he was still in the craft, which was now a mass of crumpled, tortured metal, and that they were no longer in space. Some kind of world was out there.

He saw more clearly now, through the shattered portholes, the bright flashes of blue light, much like lightning but vastly wider, brighter. It was raining out there. Or snowing. Or sleeting. He couldn't tell what, but the falling flecks seemed blue—distinctly blue, beyond the reflected light of the intermittent flashes.

David dragged himself over to Phelps who was clear of the machinery except for his arm. His chest moved in a slow breathing pattern. Finding a long, thick metal bar, he forced it under machinery crushing the arm, then pried it up. At the same time, he pulled the arm free.

"Phelps." He drew him up to a sitting position. The mashed arm and shoulder hung uselessly at his side. David slapped his face, talked to him, cajoled, threatened. But Phelps showed no sign of life except for his breathing and the blood oozing from his wounds.

Finally David gave up and propped Phelps against a wall, used his own shirt to bandage his arm, then tried to tend to his own injury. There was little he could do beyond tying on a metal rod to serve as a splint, and wrapping his leg tight with strips of clothing.

The exertions exhausted him, and he eased himself heavily down next to Phelps. The blackness, the eerie blue flashes, the dampness and precipitation floating past the shattered porthole all contributed to his deeper and deeper depression and sense of terror. The power of revenge and evil which had controlled him and directed his emotions and will to torment Phelps was now gone. His mind raced wildly from one possibility to another for escape . . . but to where, or what?

He sensed no presence of God, and felt no desire to pray. He wanted to but he felt muddied, unclean inside. He simply could not bring himself to do it, as if communication there were quite blocked off, forever, because of his foul rejection of Him in his actions of these last days.

Looking through the blackness at Phelps, he was startled as a flash of blue light suddenly illuminated his face. The man had his eyes open and was staring impassively at his companion. As David watched him, he felt a stab of new fear—of what this man might now want to do to him.

"Where are we?" the older man asked through clenched teeth, obviously fighting pain.

David stared back at the face—only occasionally visible in the flashes of light. He finally muttered, "Who knows? Some barren planet? The world beyond death. . ."

Phelps clenched his teeth harder at that. "Can't be heaven. Must be hell!"

To David, this was more than a dry jest. That precise thought had been lingering in his subconscious, and its utterance leaped in his chest like a tearing fish hook. With it was the realization that what he had accused Phelps of being—a murderer—was true of himself as well.

The thought, now in the open, possessed his mind. He had hated the fat man and Phelps. He had killed. Did God reject him? Were both he and Phelps damned souls somewhere in the stretches of hell, soon to be taken by Satan's forces to eternal torment?

"Maybe it really is hell," David said flatly.

Phelps laughed — a dry, ridiculing laugh — then started coughing. "Koehler," he said finally, "let's stop theorizing and get some sleep till morning."

"What if there is no morning?"

Phelps didn't answer, but started to pull himself up. The two of them felt their ways slowly and painfully through the twisted craft to the bedrooms, both of which were in complete shambles. But the big slabs of foam-like material on the floors were still intact, and they wearily slumped on them and slept.

David awoke first—at least eight hours later. It was still black. He stared out through the portholes, trying to piece together what was out there by the blue lightnings. Somehow the wide, bright flashes did not illumine the vast blackness.

It was then that David saw them. Two . . . then three and four, all peering into the porthole. They were different from anything he'd ever seen on earth, unmistakably serpents' heads, yet not precisely snakes. Their slender, bright-red tongues leaped in and out of their mouths, their heads weaved back and forth methodically. Nothing was between him and the creatures but a few shards of shattered "glass" remaining in the portholes.

David turned and dragged himself with all his strength to Phelps and shook him. The latter awoke groggily, but seeing the terror in David's eyes quickly glanced about the room. In a moment he was staring with equal awe and apprehension at the heads weaving in the blue flashes.

Then one started slithering in. It was large, slender and though not distinct in the intermittent light, gleaming with fantastic colors the length of its body, even over the long, slender, wing-like limbs which David would have termed shoulders.

Phelps shouted and grabbed the metal bar nearby. At that the creature began making noises sounding almost like speech. The sound was soft, liquid, melodic.

Phelps held his ground unsteadily as the serpentine body weaved along the wall toward him. When it was within two feet, a flash of light illuminated its long neck and flickering tongue and before it could make another sound, Phelps swung with a strength born of terror, bringing the full force of the bar against its long, slender neck.

The creature immediately writhed into a coil, and Phelps just as quickly swung at the moving head, smashing it right across the eyes. Then he hit again and again.

David hadn't even noticed the advance of the others. They came like a rattler's nestful through the blackness, and before Phelps had a chance to raise a blow against them, they coiled around him in a mass of colored, undulating bodies, pinioning his good arm and his legs, making their speech sounds as they encircled him.

The creatures must have weighed a hundred pounds each, and with one on each leg and a third on his arm, they easily dragged the screaming Phelps toward a porthole. Then, as David watched in horror, the bizarre shapes pulled him out of the space ship, fluttered open their long, brilliant wings and flew off with him.

As Phelps' screams died out in the blue-flashing blackness, David focused once more on the creature close to him. It's head was crushed. By the flashes, David could tell its brilliant colors were fading. Soon, in contrast with its fellows, the gems on its coat became dull, the body moved less and less. Then, if David's senses were not putting him altogether into fantasies, he watched as the creature slowly "evaporated"—disappeared in the midst of its fellows.

The creatures then started toward David. He was in the smashed bedroom and started backing toward the porthole. They were emitting their sounds again, soft, fluid, even soothing. But their forms were as naturally repulsive to David as any copperhead he'd seen at home, and he wanted so badly to shut them out, to throw something at them—to do anything!

They advanced methodically and forced David back closer and closer to the porthole. Finally he was climbing through it, his broken leg causing him excruciating pain, but pain almost irrelevant in his haste. The creatures hurried toward him, and he dropped his body out, his hands gripping the lower, broken sill which held him but cut into his palms.

As he hung from the porthole, he peered frantically below for a landing place. Far to the right he could see something like high Rocky Mountain peaks, but below it was as if the space craft were suspended on nothing or on the very lip of a cliff far, far above whatever lay below.

At the same time he felt the blue sleet-like substance falling against his body and creating strong shocks as if every particle were heavily charged with static electricity.

The creatures above were touching his hands, and he knew at that instant he could either consign himself to their wishes or plummet to whatever fate lay below.

He grimaced and released his hands.

What happened next David could not at all be sure. It seemed that he fell but a few feet and then hit some mushy substance, like the sleet, which was on a sharp angle, almost cliff-like, and slowed his descent. For at least ten minutes he rolled and sprawled down the sharp incline until he finally slid to a stop and blacked out.

When he awoke, David lay there for some time, numbed, trying to regain a touch of sanity. He moved his hand, feeling the substance on which he lay. It was like soft-frozen sludge— yet the strange fact was that everything was warm. Almost hot in fact, including the air and the unpleasantly charged blue particles which kept drifting down. He soon became extremely uncomfortable—long before his splinted leg began coming out of its numbness and the real pain began.

The blue flashes, which he now began to think of as heat lightning, remained the only source of light. Without them, the blackness was so complete that David could not even see his fingers directly before his eyes.

During the next few days no light beyond the blue flashes ever came. He was conscious only of the pain in his swollen leg, the high temperatures, his hunger, and the nasty little particles which never stopped falling.

Yet all this was endurable. What was not endurable were the terrible uncertainties, the ominous forebodings. By the third day David was convinced that he was quite literally in hell.

The conclusion was the only one logical to his mind. He knew he was being sought by the snake-like creatures he had eluded—on three separate occasions they had come, fanned out, obviously sweeping the area. He had narrowly avoided detection by burrowing a tiny hiding place in the hard sludge which covered everything, including the huge mountains. This world fitted the description he would have given of hell except for the notable absence of flames—but he was sure that the numerous hot lakes of soggy blue mush—with loathesome dark-blue spots like radiator sludge floating on them—were just as painful and repulsive. He constantly heard strange noises, including terrible shrieks, and once sensed a huge, moving blob of some kind, oozing over the terrain.

But most of all he was convinced this was hell because of the deep emptiness he felt inside. It is impossible to describe the horror of a man who looks toward the next week or next month or year for a brighter future, but can envision only his tormentors using him for food for their evil desires. He could not call out to God because he believed it was too late.

He wondered whether he would starve to death . . . what then? Endless starving to death, moving from place to place. How would that *be*? Or was he now immortal, doomed forever to suffer these pains in his body and the terrors of the future? Forever? Forever? How could he live like this a week . . . but forever? What *did* that mean?

On the fourth day, in his pain and weeping, David finally spread himself out on the blue terrain and sobbed out his anguish to God. Whether God could hear him or not, he cried out bitterly, admitting his hatreds and his rejection of God's voice in his anger against Phelps, and pled that something—if only something—could be done to alleviate some of this, to give him some hope, some understanding. The unbelievability of a God of love refusing to hear . . . yet he'd had his choice . . . it was all over; he'd made his choice when he had sinned again and again against Phelps when maybe He could have kept him, too, from this place. The thoughts in his fevered mind and anguished prayer jumbled together into senseless, maddening hopelessness.

Yet as David continued to pray, he sensed a strange feeling within, a feeling he'd known before—with Pélu, and in the library that day. He felt a filling of some of the emptiness inside.

And that feeling—that knowing—that God was responding to him was far more delightful than the cessation of pain would have been, or light suddenly appearing, or any direct answer to change his present situation. For here was hope kindled in his chest. Here was a hint of some future other than this horrible state.

A great sense of gratitude touched him, that God would still hear, that it wasn't too late, and he wept great shuddering sobs of relief.

He prayed on. It was his only touch with reality. He prayed for hours, even praying for Phelps and people on earth. He

(101)

had doubts as he did that—a soul in hell praying for people? Absurd. Was he in hell? He prayed against his doubts, for this new hope was all he had.

It seemed that he was receiving almost a direct command to dig down, dig deep into the blue, warm sludge on which he lay. Yet he had no tools but his comb and keys.

The impulse was so strong that he began. He was very weak. It was slow going, but eventually he had a hole four feet deep and found a major advantage already. The charged particles were not falling on him at the bottom, and it was a trifle cooler.

He continued digging. But at nine feet he couldn't toss the mushy chunks up out of the hole. Exhausted, he knelt on the floor of it and decided to loosen some more chunks, then sleep.

It was then that his hand felt something solid—the first really solid thing he'd found on the planet. He clawed away the warm mush around it and found it to be something like a root, yet perfectly rectangular, and blue like everything else in this world. Digging around it, he tried to follow it with his fingers, but he could do this for only a few inches, so he tried to dig below it.

David had pushed through only a short way when he felt a chunk of the material give way and disappear. He firmly grasped the solid blue rectangle and kicked with his foot. Suddenly he crashed through, and in the next instant he found himself dangling by the root or whatever it was above a surrealistic vari-blue-colored world about fifty feet beneath him.

Growing up into the roof of this subterranean world were thick, perfectly rectangular, deep-blue trees. They looked like so many pillars in a Greek structure, all supporting a roof—from which he was dangling.

David's grip was loosening. Below him was what he took to be a tiny lake, but he had no mind to try its temperature, depth, or solidity. Luckily one of the huge trees, with a great many square-leafed branches, was quite close, and a branch, free of the roof above, was near enough for him to swing his good leg over, then get a hand on it.

In his weakened condition, he was never quite sure he

wouldn't fall at any moment. But that special strength which comes at the threat of death kept him pulling from branch to branch till finally he was on a very thick, secure branch near the main trunk, perfectly horizontal to it as if the tree had been made by a carpenter. Yet alive it was, for fruit was scattered on it, square, soft, and blue, about the size of a cantaloupe. He tried one. His mouth puckered at the taste—but it seemed edible enough.

Before long David had consumed a half dozen of them. Then he worked his way down. He hadn't been on the ground for long, stretched out exhausted, before he developed a bad stomach ache. Yet he was able to keep the food down, and was soon feeling a bit of his strength returning.

He slept, then, for many hours. And when he awoke, he ate more of the fruit. He was delighted to discover that the water in the little lake was cool enough to refresh him, so he washed himself and even dared to drink from it.

This new world is quite a change, David marveled as he lay on his back, staring around at it. The place seemed limitless in distance, stretching out as far as he could see, except for small walled sections which he guessed to be the sites of the scummy, hot lakes. But down here, sparkling blue walls encased them.

That was the word to describe everything here—sparkly, in every shade of blue imaginable. No other color was to be seen. He would have thought it an illusion of the light, but his own clothes were still green and brown and his flesh retained its natural color. It was like a blue winter wonderland with 70-degree snow.

In the weeks to follow, David was to find much more to this underground world. He regained strength, but his unset leg would not heal and sapped much of it. Yet he could explore, and found a great variety of creatures, all quite different from earth animals, all without any fear of him. None were so different that he would have been surprised to find them in an obscure part of a zoo, except for their universal blueness. And some were transparent so that he could see their veins and vital organs through the skin. Plants, too, abounded, and he found quite a variety of edibles, including exotic nuts which became the most important part of his diet.

During this time he had established an excellent communication in prayer, and he was in very good spirits, considering the unknowns in his situation. He committed them to God and began trusting him far more than he ever had on earth.

He knew very little fear in this bright, idyllic underworld, until he sensed one day (or night—there was a constant illumination) that the same thing which had so terrified him up above was oozing through the forest down here.

David stared in horror. It had to be a mile wide, and was not blue but a brilliant red, like an alien in this world. He could not have described it as anything but a blob—a rolling oozing, gigantic semi-solid mass spreading over everything in its path except the trees, which it simply spread around. David presumed it was feeding, and at the same time knew he could not escape with his leg in its swollen, painful condition.

He looked frantically for a way out. All the nearby trees had branches much too high. There were no lakes close enough.

Five feet away was a small hole, and David wielded the stick he had been carrying as a crutch and attacked it, digging furiously. If he could bury himself and maintain a pocket of air. . .

The red thing moved ominously closer, and David dug still more furiously, wondering if the thing were possibly watching him even at that moment, laughing at his puny efforts. But, of course, blobs wouldn't laugh. To come to this—to be food for such a loathsome creature. . . .

The redness was becoming the dominant color before him as he hacked at the soft, clay-like substance. The blob was at least six feet high and almost on top of him. At the last possible moment, he burrowed into his shallow foxhole, then clawed the "dirt" back upon him. When he felt somewhat covered, he lay there, inert.

Minutes passed. He could feel the heat of the living thing passing over him. Air was becoming stale. He hoped it would be over soon.

Then, suddenly, he felt himself being sucked up, out of his flimsy shelter, and being engorged into it like a fragment of food into a giant amoeba.

9

As David felt himself being pulled horizontally toward the vitals of the thing, he became enfolded in the soft walls of a channel. It was as if he had been swallowed, and peristaltic action were moving him along. The comfortableness of it reminded him of a spider's soft web and a sleep-inducing injection.

There was plenty of air to breathe. It must have been at least fifteen minutes that he was moved along in this manner. Then he arrived at what he surmised to be the stomach, for before him were dozens of animals, plants, fruits, and even mineral rocks. The live creatures were all placidly sleeping or nibbling on vegetation which had been sucked in with them. All were on a soft but flat floor with covering overhead. Surprisingly, there was light. It was as if they were all relaxed on some giant's tongue, with the vast covering of the roof of his mouth above. The animals seemed to consider it a pleasant situation, but David expected darkness and gastric juices to engulf this little world at any second.

It was three hours before there was any change. Then, as easily and quickly as lifting off in a jet, David felt himself and his surroundings airborne, the entire blob apparently flying. He had the feeling they were accelerating to high speed.

He struggled over to the walls and dug his fingers into them. They were soft, but resilient. Reaching into his pocket, he dug out his keys and scraped with them. He managed to break through a thin layer of what he presumed to be membrane, but his efforts were obviously having no effect on their flight.

Finally, David felt the sensation of rapid descent, and in a few moments they were still. Almost immediately the soft material on which his weight rested began separating from the center, exposing a soft-green substance two feet below. Soon, his original floor was nearly gone, and he had to jump down to the green one. He was now out of the blob, and as he looked up, he saw the entire structure rising above him and enfolding upon itself. He was able to see ribbing in the main trunk which looked metallic . . . but before he could see more, the entire thing was a neatly wrapped package, like a Boeing 707-size bat on the ceiling.

Yes—in his fascination with the blob, he'd hardly noticed the fact that he was now in a vast building of some kind, domed, with a transparent, glazed covering. It was huge— several acres certainly—and everywhere he looked there were variations in size and shape of undulating green projections from the floor, all in the same styrofoam-like covering. Everywhere there were instruments, apparently miniaturized to a phenomenal degree and of such design that David could think of nothing similar he had ever seen—sort of an Oriental look, yet with Easter Island primitive simplicity. It was as if he were standing in America's most advanced 1999 space laboratory on the moon, but with a totally foreign motif.

He noticed, after a time, that the entire floor was moving slowly toward what he took to be the center of operations—a wide rectangular diameter all the way across the round structure. He wasn't sure whether he should turn and flee to the outer edge or not. Since he had arrived here, he had been aware of certain white-and-red flashes, whether of heat or light or electricity he wasn't sure. But if he were already being photographed or X-rayed or whatever, he probably had little chance of escape.

At first he kept moving away from that enigmatic platform, but finally, tiring, he allowed himself to move slowly beneath the low-hanging walls which separated it from the outer area.

He was sitting as he moved under the wall, and that is why from his vantage point David saw the other first. A tall, dark man was bending over one of those strange, translucent creatures. The man was making sounds which David presumed were speech, but very alien to his ears.

The tone of his speech was companionable, almost gay. His clothes were form-fitting, brightly colorful—almost Dali-esque in pattern—and what little he could see of his face made David think of a strikingly handsome young Puerto Rican or Mexican, except that he was a deep, very deep blue.

Though he knew nothing about the person before him, a

(106)

great surge of relief coursed through David as he painfully rose on his one good leg, holding the wall for support. He called out to the man.

The voice surprised him, and he stood and turned in David's direction. But as soon as he saw him his expression changed from one of surprise to a distinct expression of incredulous concern. He bounded over to the earthling, addressing him with the same sounds he had been using on the translucent quadruped. David's response in English caused him immediately to switch to thought-communication.

The blue man's whole frame of reference and set of questions seemed exotic and almost irrelevant. David had trouble separating them into meaningful questions he could answer. The other sensed this quickly and conveyed his thoughts more specifically and slowly to the earthling, at the same time examining his swollen leg with a look of perplexity on his face.

"This swelling, discoloring," he thought to David. "What cause?"

"It was broken." David spoke his words, at the same time clearly thinking them to his benefactor. "Weeks ago, when our craft smashed into this world."

The man knitted his brows in perplexity. "Why all this time? Why did you not ask? Is there a cause?"

David couldn't understand his perspective at all, though he tried to absorb the thoughts flooding into his mind. "I couldn't do more than splint it," he replied. "No medications. Constant aggravation."

Both tried to communicate further on it, and finally the dark stranger asked, "May I ask for you?"

David nodded, and at that the man began a strange procedure. He held the injured limb, looked up, and began something which seemed as much emoting as thinking. Yet David was able to be caught up in the thoughts which drew him up and up . . . lofty thoughts and feelings of intense companionship and immediate closeness to some higher power here. . . . Was there a planetary ruler here with whom he could communicate in this way?

The immediacy of this communication was so intense that it was as if they were becoming part of this force, infused with an energy he could not understand, a flood of power from an immense Niagara Falls generator, but a power more personal, meaningful, exhilarating.

The man stopped abruptly, removed the splint, and they both looked down at the leg.

It looked perfectly well.

David gingerly moved it, then kicked out with it as he felt the strength there. He leaped to his feet, still buoyant from the powerful experience.

"Who did this for me?" he asked his benefactor.

David could not quite make out the name being pronounced —something like E•AHL•OUL•. The man's speech patterns were exotic, unearthlike.

"Is he here on this planet?"

"Of course." The man again looked perplexed, as if David were asking childish questions. It frustrated him, so David changed the subject.

"What will you do with me?"

With that, more of the gay personality of the man came through. "I have never before had a man in my laboratory. Label you first?" he asked, as if it were a very large joke.

Obviously the blob had been a collecting device for his biology work. David smiled a bit weakly, and the other laughed in high spirits. "Home. Right now. My love and my small ones will be overjoyed when they see you."

They walked over to what David presumed was a vehicle of some sort. Nothing in his experience on earth could have fully described it. In style, it was a bit like a simplistic, inverted mask from primitive islands—solid black, yet with a wood-like grain. David thought it seemed poised like a Ford Mustang, but four times larger, an uncanny beauty about it, with no wheels, no obvious means of locomotion.

The inside was simplicity itself, yet the material of the panels, consoles, and sides gave it a stunning beauty. The wood or metal fairly spoke its display of warmth, richness, depth. There were no seats. Outside, the entire vehicle had been ebony black. But with the sides now closed David could see right through the roof and sides, as if it were one-way glass.

And soon he saw through the bottom. By manipulating a flat, envelope-size device shaped something like a snowflake, the man guided the craft up and forward with sudden acceleration. David at first braced himself, but strangely, they were not swept off their feet. Inside, it was as if they hadn't moved.

Somehow they whisked right through the dome of the laboratory—probably through a movable section, for David had noticed wide ribbing in one place—and flew through the underworld fantasy land of twinkling blue and square tree pillars holding up the snow-like sparkling sky.

After traveling a few miles through varied countryside, they came to the edge of a very deep depression. Here more than just trees held up the roof of this strange sub-world. A huge network of non-natural beams precisely simulating the rectangular tree trunks arched up and in and out, supporting what looked like a geodesic dome miles across in diameter. It sheltered a vast series of valleys and mountains below, and free fluids composing a river, lakes, and waterfalls.

The vehicle dipped quickly into the valley, still flying at high speed, past lovely blue hills with blue waterfalls and canyons and timber areas of the square trees reaching up, touching only the free air.

"Quite an achievement for your people to have structured this fantastic dome over the valley," David commented, very much impressed, with a feeling akin to that of seeing the Rockies. It was not only the vast heights which awed him, but also the unique beauty, like the flaming foliage of a New England autumn, but all in mosaic blues.

Thoughts were entering David's mind from the man, succinctly explaining that he alone had erected the beams, gouged out the valleys, run the courses for the waterways, imported the trees from other worlds to create this entire sub-world below the stinging heat of above. It was something like flying over New York in a helicopter and being told by the pilot that he had constructed all the buildings and bridges and raised the island itself. Yet somehow David could not doubt the man.

"How long did it take?"

The man's response was specific—but not specific to David because he had no idea of this recording of time. The thought conveyed seemed like several centuries. Yet the man looked no older than twenty-five.

After topping a high ridge, they buzzed a waterfall and then came around the hill to what was evidently the largest valley of all. Situated at the very top of the highest mountain was a structure of immense size and beauty. It was nestled snugly in a forest of multi-colored trees, like a dream castle in the Bavarian Alps. Square spires rose with the trees and above them, reaching up toward the dome-sky. David could tell his host was overjoyed to have someone with whom to share this.

They sped directly toward the home. What struck David even more than the grandeur of the place was its distinctive look, simplistic, yet unique in its broad patterns and designs of wings and sections.

The spunky little vehicle flew directly at a wall of the house, and David's reflex actions almost landed him on the floor. But by whatever trick of absorption or flexible openings, they were instantly inside the home in an area large enough for a dozen Cadillacs. Actually it housed numerous vehicles of assorted shapes and sizes—some very small and obviously for a child. The floor had the same styrofoam-green effect. Everywhere depressions showed on the wall. David got the idea they would drop appropriate tools out of some lower slot if one were to press them.

They descended a passageway lined with jagged-but-polished blue timbers and emerged into a large but strangely cozy room with an entire side opened up to the ground-level view. Within the room, in about six levels, thick fur-like carpeting invited David closer.

But the man led him through an archway which presented a hundred-yard ramp of inlaid squares of blue wood leading to the house rising about 60 yards before them. They walked up, wind blowing in their hair, the taller trees within touching distance even at the top. As they entered, David saw in the huge entranceway gigantic shapes making up a cathedral-sized musical instrument with sections something like bells and pipes and even violin contours. His guide noticed David's wonder, stepped to his left, and suddenly David heard music, alien but waterfall-soothing, as if the forests and wind and all nature itself were playing through the gigantic instrument.

Winding and rising through room after room of the home, he loved the variety: small studies where one walked in as if into a cave with the only seating in snug little inviting coves; open flying porches jutting way out from the main structure of the house, protected by translucent material. Throughout, square blue trees and imported round saplings which looked like birch and hickory grew right through the rooms and halls. Complementary flowers bloomed on and around the giant slabs of rock with which the house had been made as an organic part.

The color scheme was bright and gay, a lively but tasteful blend of ingenuity with warmth . . . a soft, flowing perfection, like a brilliant tropical flower, complete in itself as a whole, but each facet distinct in itself.

At the top section of the home, David saw a woman, dressed much like the man in form-fitting blue. Upon seeing them, she shoved something back into the wall and walked toward them. David saw on her face a look of surprised delight. His initial observation was that she had much the same gay personality of her husband—unlike Pélu who had seemed more serious, more reserved.

She spoke to her husband in that speech like ripples of water, flowing, lacking consonants. David could not enter their thoughts, but then she turned to him and spoke, conveying her meaning into his mind, one of great welcome and ecstasy that he had come. Her sincerity flowed with the thought patterns.

Then they whisked him off to another area of the house where several of their children were playing. They were dressed like their parents, but with distinctly different colors. At the sight of the stranger, a teen-ager walked up to greet him, talking in his native tongue which was still quite unintelligible to David. On a word from his father, he started thinking his thoughts to the stranger as he spoke—but not without some difficulty. Obviously, this was a talent one had to learn.

A two-year-old was happily ensconced on David's foot, looking up at him with very appealing wide eyes and a curious smile. He too started speaking, with a very limited vocabulary but apparently quite intelligent meaning. David surmised from the children's chatter that they were supremely happy just then. Whether it was because of his appearance or it was merely their usual state, he couldn't tell.

The smaller children's room—or rooms, for there was quite an expanse of space devoted to them—was a fantasy-land including all sorts of the creatures of their blue world, both living and sculpted, plus many forms of creatures David thought were somewhat like the imaginary elves and trolls of earth—but from this indication, evidently did live on other planets.

"How many children do you have?" he asked.

"Six—living with us," answered the woman. "We have others who are now adults, helping us to people this planet."

"What are your names? I need to call you something. Mine is David."

They made their rippling sounds in response, repeating their names again and again. But no matter how he tried, David couldn't begin to form the words.

"May I name you—all of you?" he asked, grinning, caught up in the infectious good will of the family. "Sir, I'll call you Paul. Okay?"

The man reminded him of a happy-go-lucky Puerto Rican student he'd known by that name. The man nodded assent, as did the others when he called the mother Lois, the oldest boy Ricky, then Stephen, Annette, Johnny, Joane, and Ted. The adults had little trouble forming the name "David" on their own tongues, or Paul or Lois either, after a bit of practice. The youngsters were not as adept.

Although there were countless aspects of the home which mystified the earth visitor, the hosts scarcely stopped to explain any of the mechanical wonders of the place but concentrated on the aesthetics of color and design—as if David knew as much about the "mere mechanics" as he did about a pencil. However, David often stopped and asked questions which they answered in detail, whatever their surprise at his ignorance.

One whole section of the home housed an extensive education/recreation area. It soon became clear to David that here the two were synonymous. Learning was great sport both to the children and the adults. He supposed there was absolutely no end to the millions of total 3-D TV presentations available in their micro-library. The children themselves could turn to any subject of any time and place, and suddenly the entire room was filled with colors, smells, atmosphere, and sounds of some historical happening or scientific phenomenon or geographic wonder. David stood in fascination—and to his surprise, his hosts, who must have used the machines constantly, expressed the same kind of wonder and excitement.

However, there were no voices of explanation in these presentations. One can speak at only about 100 words per minute. Here, thoughts rushed out at 1,000-5,000 w.p.m. rates, and David simply could not keep up with them.

After they toured the kitchen facilities, which consisted of a vast range of selector panels and hidden heating and chilling devices, they entered a large "creativity" room in which both the man and woman worked in developing or constructing anything from ingenious machines to interior decorations to three-dimensional paintings. Finally, they walked to the outer edge of the room which seemed to float into space high above the blue trees below.

Suddenly, as they walked beyond one partition, David drew himself back in horror at the sight of a creature behind it. Unmistakably, it was one of the serpent-creatures, and it weaved its head at David on discovering him, and started moving toward him. David could not suppress a cry of fear, but the creature continued to advance. The man stepped between them, his mind probing that of the earthling in complete mystification. David tried to explain to him, but it was obvious as he communicated his feelings that this "man" had never experienced fear and could not fathom David's loathing of the creature, now coiled back, still weaving its head. The host explained that it was a member of the household—like a pet, David surmised—but an intelligent and integral part of the family, even capable of speech. David still could not discard his strong revulsion.

They moved on, and David met dozens more of their pets, many of whom could speak some language or other, but all of whom apparently were of a lower order than Man, who held the supremacy over them by his creativity and intelligence.

At the evening meal they sat on the soft floor around a slightly raised, flexible plateau with various curved sections, much like carvings in the pieces of a puzzle, and quite appropriate to sit in. Each person brought out his own food by punching the appropriate selector buttons which were included in an encyclopedic electron selector, calorie rated, at each place. A magnificent variety of cuisine began appearing on the table from small trap doors. Nothing was in a container. Whether liquid or solid, small or large, the vari-colored and multi-shaped foods were coated with an edible, saran-wrap type of substance, which held the foods in small units. Once, David bit into the side of a liquid container and spilled about a cup. Most of it fell on the green table and was instantly absorbed.

The table talk about this utopia was exceedingly pleasant, for David did not want to get into a discussion about earth, and he felt if he could keep asking the questions, he could avoid the unpleasantry of explaining certain things for a time. So long as they talked about their world he stayed in very good spirits.

With an exception. At one point he asked, "If so many of these animals are intelligent household pets, which of them on the planet are used for food?" David felt it unfortunate that they were receiving at that moment his full thoughts instead of just the words, for they got his mental picture of sizzling steaks and cured ham and breast of chicken. Such thoughts were appalling to them, or perhaps more accurately, they were utterly incomprehensible and unthinkable, as if he had just suggested they carve up the little boy and boil him in a pot at the center of the table. To eat the quivering flesh—it was a crude fantasy, impossible because dead bodies did not exist here. At death, they explained, all living creatures simply evaporated, or were disembodied, into the next dimension to more glorious states of being. David quickly moved on to other questions, but he could tell that in their minds there were many questions about his world they wanted to ask.

He learned that this couple had come to this planet several hundred years ago from their home sphere which their parents had civilized and peopled long before. They had discovered the planet, explored parts of it, taken up the challenge of taming it and peopling it.

At first it had been barren, inhospitable. They had lived in their space ship for a dozen years, formulating plans, figuring out ways to make the planet viable, livable. Their underworld, supported by the imported trees from a far distant planet (Paul had found the information in his electronic compendium) was the result of great labor. Each tree had to be planted individually—by machine, of course—and the principles for the atmosphere and vegetation had to be carefully calculated, with the right animals and crops imported.

The challenge of civilizing this planet—and peopling it with millions eventually, with these first two as patriarch and matriarch—was the immediate goal. It loomed before them as a constant expression of fulfillment, and as they expressed it, an extension of the creativity of E•AHL•OUL• in themselves.

During the meal, several of the animals with transparent skins wandered in to play with the children. David smiled at their antics, but eventually, when a serpent glided in on his long, delicate wings to the boy and playfully coiled himself around him, he could barely hide his disgust. Yet he forced himself to look at the creature. No doubt it was beautiful—more striking in its beauty than any earth creature David had ever seen.

The only way he could describe it was to think of a snake as being a dried-up, desecrated mummy of this creature. Though its face was unquestionably the shape and suggestion of a serpent's, it was not, as David stared at it, repulsive in itself—only in its similarity to the earth serpent. He thought of disgusting, blackened mummy heads he had seen—shrunken, teeth showing, human and yet a mockery of a beautiful human face. Here was the original beauty of the earth's mummy-serpent.

And the skin! Compared to this, the designs on an earth snake were like a burlap beginning pattern with the rough indications of where the bright-colored threads should be. This creature coiled around the boy was like the finished product. Exquisite, fantastically sparkling jewels like diamonds and pearls made up an effect more colorful than any bird of paradise or painted desert sunset he'd ever seen. It was as if the earth snake were stripped of its gleaming gems and shrunken into a blackened skeleton of its true self. The neck was a long swan's neck, moving gracefully, beautifully, instead of twisting repulsively like an earth viper.

He looked over at his host and hostess, and felt a trifle embarrassed that they had been following his full thoughts all this time. They seemed perplexed by it, but began answering questions about their planet as he resumed his questions.

"And what have you named it?"

The melodic ripple of sound the man gave in reply he could not repeat. David suggested, "I'll give it an extra name. How about 'Blue Eden'?"

They shrugged their shoulders agreeably, as they had seen him do. Then they asked, "But what about your planet?"

He smiled. "They say it, too, was once an Eden. A green one."

"Where?"

He was at a loss to explain from this frame of reference, for he had no idea of his location now.

They rose from the meal and went to the leisure room where Paul showed him vast maps which had no relevance to him whatever, of billions of unfamiliar stars and planets and civilizations and peoples.

"We were heading for the quasars—brilliant points of light beyond any sun's brilliance, and then a terrific explosion occurred. We awoke here."

"We?"

"Phelps and I." It was the first time he had seriously thought of the other. "Another like myself. Somewhere on this planet."

The other registered no great concern but said simply, "We must find him. . . ."

As they continued looking at the map, David noticed the edge of an area near Blue Eden which was simply black and most of it off the edge of the map. It was only a few thousand light years away. "What is this?" David asked.

The man and woman both looked at him in surprise. "The void, of course. The space which is in our dimension but is not, the place of the wounded ones." They acted as if he were asking about $2 + 2 = 4$.

David focused his mind on the concept of antimatter and asked if that were true. "Yes. The opposite of our world. No one can even pass through and go to that barren world—but we have heard of some of the great men being transformed by E•AHL•OUL• to pass in. But all that is mystery. Aeons from now, we will know."

The earthling stood there, staring at his blue-skinned, handsome hosts. "There—in antimatter—is my home. I was born there, on a planet called Earth."

The two reacted as if he were still misconstruing simple first-grade math, and told him it was impossible. No one had ever gone there, except those E•AHL•OUL• had changed. But E•AHL•OUL• Himself, some say, went there and returned.

"Tell me," he asked them, "is E•AHL•OUL• also known by the name of Aelor?"

The two did not know, but Paul operated a device which soon gave him an answer. E•AHL•OUL• was indeed known as Aelor, by a very advanced group of people who lived very close to the center of the universe in this dimension.

"Then," David suggested, "ask Aelor where I am from."

Both did so, and as they had their answer communicated to their beings, David sensed an awe flooding through them such as he had never seen before—even in Pélu.

"But how?" the woman asked.

"I do not know," David answered. "I do not know at all. I thought I was still in antimatter, thrown into the Enemy's place of punishment. But apparently Aelor changed our form and allowed us through the quasars.

The two were looking at him, questioning, still trying to accept this incredible notion. "My world is one of contrasts," David offered. "Of joy, but also sorrow, of pleasure but much pain, of growth but also death and rottenness, of love and hate, of joy and guilt."

The concepts were impossible for them to assimilate, even though they could read fully the mind of the earthling.

"Guilt—that you cannot conceive of, right?"

And at that moment David began to toy with a thought which started growing in his mind, the dark side of his nature feeding it, delighting in its possibilities; and at the same time David's newer nature, shrinking back at the enormity of the consequences.

There was only one way to make them know the meaning of guilt: Only if they experienced it themselves could they understand.

But if they were to experience it, would they not produce a planet as twisted and tormented as Earth? Could the foul stain of the human race's folly be transmitted here to blotch all matter as well?

David's jaw was working hard, reflecting his deep inner struggle against the desire to make these people become like himself, to tear them from their idyllic lives of unspotted joy and dynamic. Just a word of temptation to disobey Aelor in some specific thing so they could know this. Play on their curiosity. The importance of their learning. David knew it was not Satan personally urging him at this moment; it was simply his own nature wanting to bring these people to his own fallen state.

Yet as he saw in himself the vision of what chaos his one small action could wreak, he forced his mind toward Aelor, fighting against the temptation, and begged to be spared this . . . to have this monstrous thought drained from his mind.

The couple had been following the mental struggle with amazement, as if viewing a new creation. "I suppose I should warn you," David said, leaning back against a soft-glow wall light, "that I could bring these things here also, and that it would be so terrible you cannot conceive of it.

"The worst thing you can presently think of would be for all to be disembodied in some explosion, or all planets to disappear, but then you would simply pass into another dimension of joy. You have no idea what tragedy is—may you never! But allowing me to remain here and helping me may bring tragedy to you. You must speak at great length with Aelor about this."

The man spoke. "We have been—even as you have been thinking and speaking. And we will again. But now you are tired. Rest."

They showed David to a section of the home with a soft floor like a miniature rolling flow of mountains. After they left, he wearily let himself slide into a yielding valley. He was asleep almost as soon as he did.

When he awoke, he felt as if he'd slept for two nights. He felt refreshed, but a trifle headachey, and stiff. The only person at home was Paul, whom he found in the kitchen. After a breakfast of exotic fruits and liquids, the man announced that they would look for Phelps that day.

"You talked to Aelor last night?" David asked, wiping his mouth with a disposable cloth from the wall dispenser.

"Yes. Yes, we talked much. We learned much."

That was all he would say on the subject, and soon they were in his little skycar knifing through the air toward the forest.

"Any chance a blob picked him up?" David asked.

"No—I've had them all out since you first mentioned Phelps. Nothing's come in that even faintly resembles a man."

It was eerie, after leaving the high-domed valley, to fly between the trees in the low-ceilinged forest. Several times they flew right at a tree, but some automatic device veered the craft around it. For a time they seemed to be climbing at nearly a 45° angle, and then came upon what looked like twenty-foot-high swirls of soft cherry ice cream with blue-sparkle toppings situated all along the sides of the mountain. On closer view, these red swirls appeared to be dwellings, and by the time they had landed, David knew very well what kind of settlement they had arrived at.

Hundreds of the sparkling, graceful serpents were coming out to meet the man, and by their excitement and deference, it was evident indeed that he was patriarch of the planet.

David was glad at this point that he had told him the entire story of the serpent episode, and of Phelps' destroying one. He was sure to get the full story here.

Hundreds of the creatures, fluttering and twisting, made way for an especially large, graceful one which came directly to the man and engaged him in conversation which the earthling could not follow at all. Five minutes later David and Paul were airborne again—much to the disappointment of the excited serpents.

"I doubt we'll ever find him," Paul said, unusually grim-faced for his personality. "I don't know what this will mean."

"Don't they have him?"

"No. While they were trying to fly him to my home, he kicked and wrenched himself with such violence that he twisted free of two and the third couldn't bear his weight. He must have fallen half a mile."

David grimaced, and stared at the square trunks and glittering landscape whizzing by. "Couldn't they locate his body?"

The man glanced over at him quizzically. He slowed the craft down near an embankment enclosing one of the hot pools, then turned the nose straight up and smashed through the roof.

Entering the upper world of intermittent blue flashes, falling flakes, and constant darkness was to David like a pardoned man's return visit to death row. This place of his near death and terrible anxieties filled him with horror.

They searched for several hours, using powerful lights from the craft which illumined large areas, and heat-detecting devices which would have pinpointed a living being.

"Not here," the man announced. "Must be gone."

"Let's get out and look on foot precisely where you figure he should be," David suggested.

The man shrugged his shoulders, signifying the futility of the action, but put the craft down.

They exited near one of the hot lakes, and the charged particles and unpleasant associations brought an exclamation of repugnance from the earthling. He ran his finger through the greasy slime and screwed up his face.

The other was surprised. "What's wrong?" he asked, likewise fingering the slime.

David looked sharply at his host. It irritated him a bit knowing that nothing was repulsive to the man, not even wastes of any kind, that there was no putrefaction, no pain—that even the shock he was feeling became, in Paul's body, only a message to the brain, not an enforcer of action. It was as if David's body treated him like a child who had to be forced to remove himself from pain, whereas this man's body simply relayed the message and trusted him to protect himself. Apparently earthlings weren't to be trusted in that way—for a variety of reasons.

They had searched for perhaps an hour, when David saw a depression in the sludge. He ran to it. Encrusted under the falling flakes was Phelps' form, perhaps eight inches under the new-fallen precipitation.

At his exclamation of discovery, Paul came bounding over, elated and smiling, and started quickly to pull Phelps' body from his warm grave. Then he lifted him effortlessly into his arms and carried him to the craft.

"Maybe we should just leave him here . . . just as well as. . . ." Paul looked at him as if he'd quoted a silly jest, then began working on Phelps to revive him. He began praying to Aelor. . . .

After a time, he slowly rose, looking at the earthling with new understanding.

"He is gone from his body. We are to burn him," he said flatly. It was almost too absurd for the blue man, and his brows were knitted in perplexity. Yet to doubt Aelor never crossed his mind. "How could his body remain?" he asked. "How could he go into the next joy?"

"He probably didn't," David answered dryly. "Where he is neither of us know."

Paul directed the craft toward the site where Pélu's space ship had crashed.

In mid-flight, David mused aloud, "And what of me, my friend? What does Aelor say? I am an alien in your world of matter. Am I to stay here?"

"No. You will not stay. You must go to the center of our dimension where all is beginning, and you will be changed."

"Changed?"

"I do not understand either. But you cannot remain as matter."

David thought with great apprehension on these words. He wondered if he would ever see Charlotte again. And Charlotte —what *was* she thinking about his disappearance!? How long had he been gone?

They found the spaceship still balanced on a high ledge, surprisingly intact but battered and crushed in places. Paul was much impressed with it, poring over its highly advanced design.

David took out the tape and the recorder, but left his few personal things which seemed of no particular use to him here. Then they returned to the sprawling Blue Eden home.

After dinner, in the huge smelting and developing area under the laboratory, they burned the body of Phelps.

Later, alone on the soft floor, David wept.

10

After the Phelps incident, it was never quite the same in this Blue Eden. David's cutting fear that he would tempt these innocents to learn about guilt, fear, and rebellion haunted his mind. Also, he had been told that someone called "the Eshoen" would soon visit the planet to take him to the center of the universe. It frightened him.

True, he was in fellowship with Aelor, and trusted, but the thought of being brought before these beings, and maybe "disembodied". . . .

He expressed his concern one day to Paul as they were working in the laboratory. "How do I know what's beyond this dimension?" David asked, then smiled and tried to sound humorous. "I don't want to stand around playing a harp day after day, or sit on a cloud singing choruses. I'm not the type!"

David hadn't thought himself humorist enough to evoke the hearty laughter which was Paul's response.

"What *do* you like?" Paul asked. "It gives you great pleasure to shove mushy or chunky globs of material into a hole in your head. You love to bring your body next to a female biped like yourself and just sit there. You enjoy simply stretching yourself on a soft surface and leaving your body there for hours. You get exquisite delight from certain waves of molecules hitting membranes in your ear.

"I doubt," he said, smiling, "that you'll end up playing a harp or sitting on a cloud in the next dimension, but what if Aelor put such pleasurable sensations into your fingertips that you enjoyed playing the harp more than you would eating, or sex? What if cloud-sitting became the most delightful pleasure you had? Remember—Aelor put into your nerves and cells every pleasurable response, including your need and love for a woman and for children. The real you isn't the sum total of your body responses. If you are with Aelor, you are happy, often exhilarated. If he wished, he could make you enjoy wriggling your toes so much you would want to do it all the time, for thousands of years on end—and love it!"

David laughed with Paul on the last comment. "But it *is* hard," David said, "to even conceive of being happy without a female to love, children to raise, a family to share with. . . ."

"Yes, it is," Paul quickly agreed. "But is Aelor happy? Are the telora happy? Of course! We are simply made to respond to different joys. And, certainly, we are all 'family.' "

"Yet, don't your people ever get killed—in earthquakes, accidents, fires? Wouldn't your wife grieve terribly? There would be no more sharing. No more family!"

"She would rejoice in that I have gone to the greater joy . . . and will be there to greet her when she joins me. She would have many other people to live with and love, and so would my children."

After this conversation, David took more and more delight in staying on this sparkling blue planet—barrenness transformed into habitation—and in learning from these people. It was astounding what individuals freed from the ordinary frustrations of self-direction were able to accomplish as they moved in constant energy from the Source of Power itself. No emotions dissipated it. David had read of scientists saying that even the most brilliant men on earth used only 4 percent or less of their potential powers. Here everyone used 100 percent of his potential! And David sensed that he could live the same way, if he would just yield himself more and more to the power he was experiencing here. He felt bound more and more to Paul and Lois and their children, primarily because of this force within them, and now in him. Yet he felt like such a fledgling in it all, as if he were appropriating such a small bit of the magnificent power and love available.

There was never lack of activity for these people. The conquering of the planet (which he learned was far larger than earth), the learning of new sciences and languages, the education of the children, the creating of exotic, colorful new foods in a thousand appealing shapes or new fabrics and designs for clothes—all were challenges to be met. And their persistence and ingenuity were linked in a very personal way with Aelor.

There was discipline in the home, but by nature the children were compliant to the parents' wishes. They slept little, ate

(123)

well, never had the smallest argument or least disappointment.

It was almost *too* utopian. Yet, David mused, he supposed a starving Hong Kong refugee who had never known anything but the most abject poverty could barely understand—*really* understand—how a man would live in opulent suburbia. Of course, this was a far greater jump—from wealthy suburbia to this. It was like a fairy tale. But they were living it, and it seemed far more real to David now—*far* more real—than the blackened shades of the world called Earth. He wasn't sure he wanted to go back.

Probably the most enjoyable activity for David was the games. With the total 3-D communications available, Paul introduced him, on his large playing court, to dozens of friends from other planets. They seemed to be standing right there—in full perspective—although there was no substance to their bodies. They could walk right through one another. Yet with a sensitized "ball" (actually a flat, square wafer) which responded to blows from either side, they were able to play a great variety of games no less exciting than football or jai alai.

A few games involved the elementary concepts of separate goals toward which they drove the wafer. But there were myriads of variations—spinning it around an opposing player for a score, or leading the players into certain forbidden formations which counted them out. Some of the games took such a high degree of mental gymnastics that David simply could not keep up. But after he would lose for their team, Paul would good-naturedly laugh and bounce him around.

Actually, less than a fourth of the games involved competition against one another. Most often they competed against nature itself, to conquer a very difficult feat as a team. Sometimes they would play for several hours trying to overcome one difficult setup, persistently, energetically driving with all their powers.

And at the end, David would be waiting on the sidelines and Paul would come over exhausted, yet never uncomfortable, his coal-black, wild mane of hair drooping all over the sides of his head. After swimming in one of the pools, he would put his head into a small compartment of the wall. A grooming device combed his hair into place in a rugged style unique yet neat, and clipped the hair at the same time.

David could have written down the details and plans for scores of such ingenious objects, yet as he thought of his homeland and what he would like to communicate down there, all these wonders seemed irrelevant to the basic issue: the source of all these things. He wanted desperately to communicate the magnificence that most earth men rejected.

David had heard expressed many times the thought, "Construct a universe with no trouble in it and you make it impossible for man to develop his finest moral qualities—patience, endurance, compassion for suffering." He'd often heard the analogy of a painting needing blacks to give it depth, and humans needing suffering and pain to become people of depth.

Yet these people were morally far, far superior to him. Because they were innocent of evil, the moral force of the universe flowed through them. He became quickly convinced that a pain-racked, hate-and-fear-filled world was not necessary for humans to rise to their potential. The only thing necessary was Aelor. Persons in an evil-free universe were free to choose—and would always choose God. They could remember Satan if they wanted to know the consequences of self-will. And maybe Satan's and Earth's epic was the only black on the canvas of the universe, the only cancer to be sliced away, so that all would know . . . but never think of trying it themselves.

David wondered how he could communicate this on Earth. He sketched out little articles and books he'd like to write. One would be entitled *The Great Invasion*—how Aelor-ké entered the heartland of the enemy to wrest from him doomed men . . . he wanted desperately to convey somehow what Christmas really means. He wanted this as much as he wanted to see Charlotte. Yet he didn't know if he would ever see her again, and this specific thought haunted his mind.

* * *

One day Paul sought out his friend and declared, "You need a challenge. Come. Let's explore."

David thought they would use the small craft and fly around the planet. But instead they walked out to the laboratory. Five levels down was a huge hangar which held a flat, oblong ship about 150 feet long.

They entered and David found it distinctly different from Pélu's craft, especially in the design of the interior. There were four control seats at the front with a large sheet of see-through metal (David had observed no portholes whatever from the outside), and as they seated themselves, it was obvious that this was the front of the ship, to be maneuvered with the control console before them just like a terrestrial jet.

David was amazed at the ease with which the craft left the planet. Paul simply pushed one button and without any other activation the craft shot through a channel in the building, up through the blue-flashing atmosphere and out into space.

"You didn't even have to start it," David observed. "Thruster runs all the time?"

"Sure! Fuel is this big," he smiled, indicating the size of his fist. He was speaking English now, even matching David's gesticulations and using his concepts of measurements and time. "Lasts for milleniums. Only eight known planets in all of space have it. Other kinds of fuel are twenty times as large for the same power."

"Paul, where are we going?"

"To a nearby planet. I've explored only small sections of it. We'll go to the far side. No human has ever been there—as far as I know."

"You say 'human,' " David said, staring at his blue-skinned companion. "Yet we are not of the same creation—are we? Our people had one ancestor—Adam. Surely your race could not have sprung from ours."

Paul shoved the flexible seat back and stared out into the star-speckled blackness. "No, we are a separate creation. We are not, as you say, *homo sapiens*. Of that I'm fairly certain. But we are on the same level. The ileo—or telora as your Pélu called them—are a little higher, more intelligent than we. The serpents are a little lower."

The man looked at the earthling with a shrug. "That is about all we know . . ." Obviously, he was asking David to supply information about Earth. But David had shrunk away from that. Somehow it didn't seem necessary to have to explain about things like war and murder and divorce and sadism . . .

"If Aelor were to find this thing you call evil in us . . ." Paul began.

David interrupted. "You know, of course," he started, "that Aelor himself went to antimatter. He did so to wage a terrible battle against the Enemy and his powerful forces which rule there. Man, controlled by the twisted powers, took him, drove spikes through his hands, his feet, drained the life from him. And he knew pain—knew it more terribly than any human ever had, for he carried the punishment for every evil there is . . ."

At this Paul was staring at him full in the face.

"Yes," David continued, "Aelor himself became a man, was slaughtered because we'd done wrong. Slaughtered so we could once more become like you."

For the first time in his life, the real shame of it caused David's cheeks to flush. Here he was, the representative of that race, just as guilty as any other human, and he had to admit to another being what his evil actions had caused. He looked down, then said, "If Aelor were to find evil in you? I don't know," David mused. "I really don't know. It couldn't be that he would have to die again. Could it be that in some way that death on earth was the pivotal point for all time, for all dimensions, the center from which all time and space and dimensions flow? . . ."

Paul sat without answering for some time. Finally, he ventured, "It could be the pivotal point. But if his death covers all to bring us back to himself, why cannot the Twisted One himself be redeemed?"

"I really don't know. He was not tempted by someone else —his sin was his own," David half asked, half answered. "He rejected God—the same as most humans do."

Paul looked at him sharply, and it took David a second to understand his puzzlement. Then, "Yes, it is true. Most humans reject Aelor and side with the Twisted One. He has a powerful hold on them through their own natures which are much like his, unless changed by Aelor-ké."

They continued the discussion for the two or three hours it took to reach the planet. It seemed like dusk as they flew in— not dark, but not daylight either. They drifted down through the cloudless atmosphere, past huge, precipitous cliffs and mountains which seemed like giant slabs jutting up into the sky, with thick vegetation covering all—even the chunky

(127)

mountain tops. Great seas of thick reddish mist filled the valleys and the great flat areas.

"This is a young planet," Paul commented, pulling a lever to float the craft down into the green-and-blue vegetation below. He touched another control and the spacecraft suddenly glowed bright red in front, and long shafts of white light penetrated the mist in all directions so that they could see clearly. The red glow was from an intense heat shield, which began slicing a path for the space craft. They cut down, down through the exotic, curled vegetation.

"These trees and vines must be hundreds of feet high," David commented.

"At least a mile," Paul corrected. "They apparently never stop growing. Must be an exceptionally rich floor here to feed them."

They saw just one kind of creature, but many of them. They looked something like fifty-pound cardinals with soft plumage, but also like sleek tigers in their movements. They scurried quickly from the craft's path.

David became more and more excited as they cut horizontally through the forest in the direction of a loud roaring sound which increased in intensity every mile. Finally they broke out of the forest to a vast sea of shimmering red, extending as far as their lights could show. There was a beach of sorts, composed of some kind of animal peelings like shells—mostly deep yellow—which pushed back the forest for perhaps a quarter mile. Above the sea was the great, thick mist it generated, which had effectively hid all this from their view when they had been above.

They were able to make excellent speed flying directly above the beach in the direction of the roaring sound. At times the mile-high forest edged out almost to the red surf, so that they flew out over the sea, then back again. Then, as great billows of the red mist began enveloping them, Paul circled back and started cutting his way through the forest again along the edge of the sea.

The sound was now so deafening that he stopped the craft, settled it on the forest floor, and led David into another room.

"You're keeping it from me. What is that roaring?" David shouted.

Paul pushed him up against a square section in the wall, adjusted some dials which immediately tuned out much of the crashing sound, then answered, "You'll soon know. But first we must protect ourselves—there's no air on this planet, and a far different gravity."

He was still adjusting dials and feeding computers as David asked, "Does this craft automatically adjust? It must have been all this time."

"Yes, but keep standing just where you are, and the force fields will envelop and protect you *outside*."

"What about air?"

"A bubble of it will accompany us, held by the force field. I'll show you the details on it when we get back."

He then led David through the door and out to the floor of the towering forest. The surface was hard—very hard, almost like metal—yet the trees broke right through it, as did tough-looking vegetation of various shapes, sizes, colors. Generally, there was ample room for walking, except in a few areas of almost solid growth. Paul kept the ship following them by remote contral, at a distance.

The excitement gripped David as strongly now as it did Paul. They were treading their way through the forest on the very edge of the sea. In his shirtsleeves. David felt perfectly comfortable, yet knew that if the force fields broke he'd be crushed and asphyxiated.

He was now feeling more and more the joy of endless discovery and creativity possible in matter. On earth, limitations and impermanence plagued him. He could discover, he could create, but in such a short lifetime! So little time to do so much. Here, there was no sense of passing years, of being robbed by time. Here was unlimited space, unlimited time— only an eventual transition into a higher world in a different dimension, continually being prepared in a learning process, gradually being absorbed more and more into the Omniscient, and sharing his creativity.

Till that moment, David never realized just how much his mortality on earth had bothered him, had cast a cloud over any major plan he had ever made.

They threaded their way on between the trees, exhilarated by the strangeness and newness of the sights and the sounds surrounding them. After several miles, they broke upon the very lip of the forest ledge. Before them the vast edge of the sea, visible for miles in the billowing mists, plummeted down to what seemed a bottomless fall.

Paul fairly bubbled with enthusiasm. "I'll bet twenty-five miles straight down—at least," he declared. "The whole sea falls off here into this giant fissure."

David felt the same emotions he had had as a little boy at Niagara Falls, standing on the lip of those cascading floods. Yet the excitement here was that *they were the first on the scene,* like the Indians of old who must have discovered Niagara. And this dwarfed it by a millionfold! Here was one of the delights a man of matter could exult in constantly—exploring, finding wonders beyond imagination, making of them cities and worlds. David knew that in that moment he had escaped the limits of his own species and had been immersed in a new element of meaning.

They stood there overwhelmed. Finally, after Paul had retrieved a fist-sized chunk of the forest floor, broken up by a growing tree, they reluctantly re-entered the craft, flew out over the billowing mists and left the planet.

"Isn't it delightful," Paul said on the return trip, "that Aelor has not finished the worlds himself?"

David smiled. "What do you mean?"

"He lets us share in his making of worlds. He could have created our planet ready-made with cities, dams, power plants, walls, all that's needed, and everyone perfectly educated. But we are 'made in his image' as you say, and we become a part of his creativity, joining with one another to make beautiful civilized worlds out of the rough material he gives us. He could as easily have kept all the joy of making to himself . . ."

When they arrived at home in the little skycar, Paul immediately bounced out of it, dashed through the garage aperture, and with a wild yell bounded over to his wife, who at that moment was playing an instrument that resembled a marimba. She dropped the sticks, flung out her arms, and the two of them embraced, spinning around.

The father was quick to re-live his explorations, to the fascination of the youngsters. They all sat around talking for quite some time. Then he held up the piece of forest floor from the planet. Everyone examined it with only mild curiosity—it was blue-gray and not too exciting. Then he pulled out a control device from a tiny pocket near his ankle.

"This chunk," he explained, "has a force field on it to give it the same density as our world. But watch the magic as I release it so that it regains its true weight.

He placed it in the center of the floor, and as soon as he twisted a dial, the rock-like substance simply disappeared right through the floor. There was a hole where it had been.

"Not only could you not lift that little thing," Paul explained, "but its density is so great it would fall right through your hand. It would be as if you took that huge boulder which is by the mountain and compressed it into this little form, with all its weight still there. The whole planet is made like that!"

After his demonstration, Paul left with his wife to go for a ride. They were apparently in a warm, romantic mood.

A thing that struck David was that the "Law of Diminishing Pleasure" didn't apply in this world at all. Passion seemed very much a part of their love, as if they were newlyweds. Paul could be as excited as a child at a thundering cascade, yet he'd probably seen wonders to surpass it.

*   *   *

During the next weeks Paul and David made frequent trips to other planets. The shock of arriving in bustling cities of commerce and communications here in matter, with advancements so dynamic and diverse, kept David alternating between delighted discovery and the desire to shrink within himself, surfeited.

It was not so much the completely automated homes nor the brilliant, fiercely undulating paintings of pure light covering huge sections of walls, nor the multileveled cities dropping into the sea for miles. It was the people. No words could come close to describing them adequately. Their utopia didn't emerge from novel concepts of economics or justice or education. It lived within them, making them whole personalities free to be themselves in the joy of Aelor.

Schools and universities were unknown. Everything was a

learning experience—the five-year-old's finger painting at home; the fifteen-year-old's math calculations to help his father build. David thought of Earth, where vast energies were expended on jockeying for power, elections, debates, graft, protests, council meetings—millions of activities to enable one to *start* accomplishing. Here even committee meetings were programmed for accomplishment!

At times, David and the family would visit a remote planet via their total 3-D "television." They would walk into the square picture area and truly "be there," as earlier visitors to Blue Eden had in playing with Paul and David. Yet, on these visits to other planets, David could neither touch nor smell his surroundings. It was as if Aelor had not allowed the ruse to be complete, so that reality would remain intact.

It was by this means that they visited a small planet where the people had little commerce and lived much like David's ancestors in the 1800's. Their homegrown bounties of food, small gardens of flowers and fruits all planted individually, offered sharp contrast to the worlds of commerce around them. But the people, who kept full communication with other worlds, loved to press their hands into the soft purple earth, plant the stony seeds, harvest the pastel fruits. No weeds choked the plants. No thorns pricked the gentle orange hands which kneaded the soil. Four hours per day were quite sufficient for labor. The rest was spent in travel, reading, discussions, love, music, painting, discovering new ideas. These vivacious people thrilled David, lifted him to new delights, but at the same time depressed him because of his own race, his own feelings. He would gladly have stayed here forever, to become a part of all this. But he was strangely out of joint with it all, fearful of his latent evil, knowing he was a speck of antimatter in matter, however miraculous his tie with Aelor.

On his final trip away from Blue Eden with Paul and his family, he understood with horror the full reality of this.

They had come to a mini-planet—really a moon of a larger planet—to attend a wedding. As the spacecraft darted in for a landing, David could see that the little spheroid was most peculiarly shaped.

They alighted to the sound of flowing music, almost Spanish with a touch of castanet-like sound, and were quickly involved with a huge crowd of people moving like a wide sea down an incredibly long valley toward a central area.

It was a long time before David understood what was here. Apparently, the small planet had been sliced to the very core, much like an eighth of an apple cut neatly out, but the material sliced out was heaped up at the lips, making the most gigantic amphitheater imaginable. The closer he got to the center, the warmer it became, and he thought he saw a burning glow at the core.

As far as he could see, people were beginning to sit in groups on the velvet moss covering the ground, tens of thousands in every direction. Dozens of neat aisles, gleaming with thick yellow moss, led directly to the core of the planet like petals of a gigantic daisy.

When they had arrived, bright, white light was illuminating everything. Now, the entire sky was changing, and the lights assumed flaring colors, all brilliant and scintillating—lemon yellows and ivy greens and sunset pinks; the music blended with it all, swirling and dancing up and over and through the little groups of people sitting everywhere around him under delicate coral-blue trees.

Suddenly, David realized that he had already sat down, entranced, and that he had become separated from his friends. Yet the delightful iridescence of the beginning pageant had him in such a mood that he cared little about that.

The colors slowly became richer, deeper, with gold, silver and white etching burgundy reds and deep sea greens and flaming apricots.

It was then that he saw a girl sitting just a few feet away from him, alone, exquisitely, beautifully rapt in the colors and music. David felt, as one feels deeply very few things in life, that human eyes had never beheld such a goddess. Words couldn't describe her—nor the emotions he felt on looking. And it seemed mere pupils and cornea and nerve systems were unable fully to relay this sight.

He felt somewhat the same emotion as when, on earth, he stood in a field staring at a fully blossomed dogwood—so beautiful it made him ache inside. Mere touching or staring at those blossoms could not satisfy the burning to share the tree's beauty.

(133)

She looked eighteen. Her long, strangely curling hair flowed around her cheeks and shoulders like flowers. Her resolute lips depicted a graceful dynamism. She was of pure ivory white, not at all like an earth Caucasian, and her hair was deep wine red. Her exotic clothes resembled, in fact, the blooms and leaves covering a dogwood, accentuating the beauty of her skin and hair and seeming to be a part of her.

"Hello," he called.

She looked over and blinked her eyes very rapidly at him. David took that to be a friendly greeting, and he smiled broadly. She returned his smile with flickering lights in her eyes and merry crinkles at the corners of her mouth. David sidled up closer to her.

"How happy to watch another joining of two into greater joy," she thought to him.

"Are you a relative of the ones to be joined?" David thought back to her. Her mind did not comprehend. "Of course," she answered. "Who is not?"

"I mean sister, cousin?"

"No. We come to many, many weddings, great distances." There was a long pause. She sat there quite comfortable with the silence, enveloped in the sounds and sights.

"Well," David began to make conversation. "I suppose you have to drag along the male members of your family to these affairs, as on my planet?" he asked, trying to sound a bit humorous.

She blinked her eyes rapidly, as if it equalled laughing to her, and then did laugh as she followed David's thoughts and expressions. "How different are your people? Are not weddings just as glorious—more glorious—for men as for women? Yours are unique ideas."

David fell silent, for at that moment all grew black, except for streaks of silver—like spider webs—rippling in the black skies. Then, as suddenly as a match flares, the air was full of bright yellows and greens and the gay, exotic music of shaking pods and rippling drums with staccato horns, all seeming to focus directly on a couple at the outer edge of the amphitheater, the head of the miles-long aisle. Colors and music sprayed from them like an aurora borealis.

David was near the couple. Both were ebony black, with

(134)

gold eyes and golden hair. The brief clothing they wore gave the illusion of fire caressing their bodies, all golden flames to match their hair and eyes. The joyous colors from the sky swept around them, sparkling up to the stars, and out to the onlookers who seemed an organic part of the spectacle. *What a beautiful bride!* David kept thinking. *What beauty!*

Then, they began singing—to each other—in vigorous ballads which mingled sophistication with earthy, exuberant emotions. It immediately shot shivers throughout David's body, and as the graceful couple walked and sang their way down that aisle, he listened intently.

After the ebony bride and groom had passed him, he began to realize that, strangely enough, he could still see their faces, their dancing walk and gestures; and then he understood that it would be that way all the way to the core of the spheroid. Some method of mirrors or whatever kept them intimately close visually, no matter where he was sitting. And, to each person in the amphitheater, the two lovers were walking down the nearest yellow-moss aisle.

David understood all this from the mind of the girl beside him. She seemed mystified that he was not familiar with these principles.

He stared into her wine-red eyes and felt the need to say dramatically, "I come from antimatter, where all is different." He could tell that as soon as he said that, she was as incredulous as if he had just announced he could separate into five people on the spot.

"How is all so different?" she asked, very much amazed at the young man beside her, yet believing because she had never doubted any man.

His mind raced, and in his chest started to grow the desire to explain. To explain perhaps too much.

"*We* are free to choose what Aelor wants for us, or something else."

"Who is not?" she asked.

He gritted his teeth and stared at the ecstatic couple before him marching to their further joy, his own emotions quite the opposite.

"You are free," he explained. "But you never choose anything but Aelor's will."

"Of course." She blinked her eyes. There was a pause. "Of course," she repeated.

He could see that it was like telling a child he would always say yes to his favorite candy—any alternative would be unthinkable—and that she comprehended nothing of his point.

"Do you not sometimes want a second piece of sweets, when there is only one there?"

"Yes, but if there is not a second, another food or another joy will replace it."

"What if your brother had the second piece of sweets you wanted? And you took it from him to eat?"

She looked at David as if he were projecting senseless riddles. To take her brother's food when he wanted it was utterly unrealistic, such as for no reason exploding the planet they sat on.

David stared at the singing couple again, and asked slowly, "Think of the love this couple will soon share. The caresses, the complete union as one. Aelor has said to them up to this day, 'Wait. Wait. Wait till my time.' But what if they had not waited?"

She looked at him, again with the feeling of his being a clever riddler, projecting nonsense to exercise the mind. David put his arm about her and asked, "Think of yourself. You get warm feelings inside when a man touches you, holds you. Now Aelor always says, 'Do not yield to those touches beyond a certain point.' But think how delightful it would be if you could, if you took your pleasures now, not always postponing them. Doesn't your body say to enjoy these feelings now?"

He kept staring into those piercing, wine-red eyes. He wanted those eyes to reflect the same haunting in his own, to know the terrible anguish of stepping away from Aelor. He couldn't stop himself in his desire for her to be like him, to understand, to be tempted and to fail.

It had little to do with sex. He was not trying to seduce her in that sense. He simply wanted her to cross knowingly the will of Aelor just once, whether it be taking a piece of fruit from her brother, or yielding to a meaningless expression of desire.

She had been thinking and now was projecting her conclusions: "Yes, of course my body says it wants a thing when

Aelor has another plan for it. But the power of Aelor is so strong it is like these great lights in the sky overpowering the tiny flame of this flower." She held up a blossom on her wrist, and David saw at the center a separate flower, small as a pearl and shaped somewhat like a snapdragon, indeed emitting a tiny, needle-like shoot of blue-and-orange flame.

David sat for a moment. Finally he said, "But what if you fed that flame and it began to consume the flower, and then the larger flower, and then consumed you and eventually this whole amphitheater, blinding out all the rest of the light in an inferno of blue-and-orange flame?"

She looked a bit perplexed and even troubled. He despised himself even as he pressed his point with, "Here in matter you obey the will of Aelor easily, because you are so used to doing so. But with us in antimatter, we obey so seldom that we have built the inverse pattern." David drew her just a little closer to him. The music was an ecstatic delirium of dancing now before them. She asked, "But what if I *would* take the other pleasure, as you do in antimatter?"

He stared at her and suddenly realized afresh that she knew nothing of the implications of this, not even what wrong meant. She surely did not understand pain, guilt, anguish. Her delight was in obedience to Aelor, the same obedience that he had been striving for. Her eyes communicated only love toward David; not erotic love, but simply the joy-love of Aelor which flowed through them all here.

That is when he almost vomited his sin out of himself, calling on Aelor for help, wrenching himself away from her and digging his fingers into the soft, yielding moss. He was horrified, terror-stricken at what he had been playing with. He felt terribly askew in this world. He wanted to escape, to return to Earth where he could wreak little additional havoc. If he were to draw down just one person here, what might it do to matter? What wars, what disease, what pain—from *his* act? He would be a Judas, a human snake in the annals of their history. And Satan was not here in him—only David's old nature tantalizing him to make another like himself.

He wept, and the mystified girl beside him merely watched, not comprehending grief, thinking possibly he was joining in his own antimatter way into the ecstasy before them.

(137)

The singing of the couple increased in intensity and they were now joined by the four parents. It seemed curious—the parents looked little older than the bridal couple. A great host of youthful friends gathered round, chanting to a near-calypso beat, and the groom himself sang before he kissed his bride. There was no embarrassment or nervousness on the part of the couple as everyone in the vast arena gazed with joy at each expression on their faces, all sharing the radiance, all becoming an organic part of the occasion.

There was no exchanging of gifts, no vows, only singing and flowers by the thousands which somehow floated around the couple in scented profusion and diversity, the music and words going on and on, as if it were an extemporaneous pageant written by the bride and groom.

And then it happened. David could not comprehend fully the wonder of it, but somehow in the core of that tiny planet, the molten center glowed brighter with a million shades and tints of mineral hues and, if David's eyes did not deceive him, the head and shoulders of a man of the same skin color and features as the couple loomed before them, from the flames. Then—brilliant light! No—more than light, for David could distinctly feel and even taste and smell it. The presence enveloped the whole planet and the voice of the fiery spectre boomed out to join in paeans of joy with the mortals. David was caught despite himself in the ecstasy of it all. A rushing, pulsating velvet rain was drenching him with love.

David had no idea how long he was caught up in all this. At last he found himself alone on the soft velvet moss, except for Paul gazing down at him, smiling.

He looked up at him stupidly. At length, he asked, "Who was the man in the center of that burning?"

"The telora of these worlds," Paul said, smiling. "Come. They're waiting."

David followed his host. But he mumbled in awe, "I am not ready for this place . . . ."

*   *   *

Four days later, after many leisure hours of "reading," thinking about Charlotte, and exploring the man-made facets of Blue Eden, Lois came to him as he was exploring the fourth floor of the laboratory. "The Eshoen are here," she announced. "They will take you."

His apprehension gripped him. "Couldn't I walk instead?" he quipped nervously.

She laughed, hardly sensing his uneasiness. "Every step you'd take would carry you further away. Remember, we are part of an exploding universe—exploding from the center. You must go enormous speeds toward the center simply to stay the same distance away from it. You will now travel millions of times further and faster than all your journeys thus far."

"Ask a simple question and you get a pageant," he laughed, trying to keep the humor of the mood. "What is it like? Have you been there?"

"No. It is too far. Come. The Eshoen wish to return quickly." There was a touch of awe in her voice, as if they were mighty creations, and a naked fear struck him that these might not be humans but some other spirit beings or ethereal powers. He trusted Aelor and communicated to him constantly now, but he couldn't stifle these fears of the unknown.

David was even more frightened when he and his hosts took an elevator to the upper world, but there were no blue flashes. David saw then why the Eshoen hadn't flown down into Paul's man-made paradise. Their space ship blocked out everything above it. All David could tell about it was that it had a flat underbelly, stretching as far as the eye could see in every direction. Certainly it was a hundred miles in diameter, a complete city in the air above them.

"My friend," Paul said, with his usual broad grin. "We will join together somewhere again in space and time. We *will* meet again."

It was like saying goodbye to a fantasy world of joy. The happiness of this couple was not the fragile thing quickly lost, but a permanence of joy between two people so idyllic he could only weep at leaving.

Suddenly he felt himself rising to meet the great expanse of metal above him.

11

Charlotte was sitting in David's easy chair in his den, Carla Adams directly across from her. A pause had developed in their conversation.

The older woman broke it. "How do *I* know? How could I know? But so help me, Charlotte, you *can't* do anything rash. You won't be simply ruining yourself, but him more than you. You can't throw away two lives like that."

"For heaven's sakes, how *can* I do anything rash? Divorce him? He's not around. Maybe he's dead. Maybe James Bond has him. Maybe he woke up during a flying saucer dream and disappeared. Maybe he's committed to a looney bin. Here I sit, listening to you telling me not to do anything rash. So I'm supposed to simply wait and wait until the polar ice caps melt and reveal the mystery?"

Carla dug her fingers a bit more into the rocker and offered, "Look, it would be absurd for me to tell you I know David better than you. But we both know he's solid. Something's happened, and we're going to have to find out precisely what it is!"

"Well, don't think for a minute *I* don't want to find out . . . but don't think for a minute that I enjoy playing these silly games. All I want is my husband back, as the same man I married. This intrigue/espionage/whatever-it-is game is not for this hometown girl. You can't tell me Mr. Carlisle is coming out here to inquire simply about David's health or even to make a pass at me or something. He realizes I'm not stupid enough to be waiting alone."

"No, he isn't stupid at all, and—"

"So, what *does* he want?" Charlotte interrupted. "I don't like this at all. You know how his men who were here before just *dripped* with curiosity about every little thing. If David were the chairman of the board, they wouldn't be *that* interested in his whereabouts or his health."

"Obviously," Carla agreed. "And for Carlisle of Arco Industries to come out here himself is rather unbelievable . . . and unpleasant."

Charlotte looked over at her sharply, but the Arco secretary did not explain.

Carlisle arrived more than twenty minutes late. He was accompanied by two of his vice-presidents, and Charlotte ushered all three into the living room. For the first ten minutes or so of his visit, Carlisle simply inquired about David, offering his "sincere concern." But when he finally came to the point, Charlotte was on guard. He began talking about scripts David had been preparing for Arco and how much they needed them now.

He said nothing about UFO reports—as the earlier visitors had done, grilling her extensively about David's comments to her about them. Carlisle insisted they go through David's things, supposedly to find the scripts he had typed.

Tenaciously, Carlisle and his men maneuvered. But Charlotte simply replied that she would look for the scripts herself while Carla kept them entertained in the living room. But the Arco president adroitly countered that only he knew precisely what he was looking for.

Charlotte felt like an animal being cornered. "Mr. Carlisle, I'd be happy to find it—there is only one drawer of his desk where he puts his office work. If it's not there, I'll look through everything else as well!"

Her back was to the door of the den now, and Carlisle was moving toward her.

How does one sense evil in a person? This man was not frowning, was not threatening, was only smiling—and advancing. But Charlotte felt that evil was fairly oozing from him. She well knew about the strange equipment in the den, and she knew about the typed report detailing how it was to be used. She had no intention of letting Carlisle get at it unless he could come up with an explanation about his interest.

"Tell me," she said, pleading with her eyes for him to explain. "What do you *really* want? I'll find it. In fact," she added, bracing her hand against the door frame, "I might even let you help me look."

"I've already told you," Carlisle said, with the impatience of a man who is not used to getting the runaround from anybody less than a corporation president. "Excuse me," he demanded, and pushed his way past her as the two vice-presidents strategically moved to block her way.

Charlotte's temper burst, and she elbowed the two men sharply, twisting her way in after Carlisle, shouting, "Who do you think you *are!* This isn't your house! Get out of here! Get your obnoxious body out of this house!"

"Come now," he remonstrated, his back toward her as he immediately caught sight of the computer on the floor. His men had again positioned themselves in her way so she could not advance, but now her blood was roaring through her veins, and she fairly screamed at him, "Damn you! This is my house!" She threw herself at the man, kicking and threatening to call the police.

Carla watched dumfounded as the vice-presidents yanked the irate young vixen off their boss, who leisurely began inspecting the document explaining the machinery and its intended use. Charlotte struggled and stamped on the feet of the men holding her, but could make no headway to get at Carlisle. She finally pulled herself away from the men, heading toward the opposite side of the den.

A moment later, Carlisle was looking into the blazing eyes of a determined young lady who held a pistol aimed directly at his head.

His immediate reaction was one of amusement, and he motioned for the men to move toward her. They started to, but when her pistol shifted to them, they stopped.

"It isn't even loaded," Carlisle said, still looking amused.

"It *is* loaded, Mr. Carlisle," Charlotte said with cold anger in her voice. "I loaded it myself, and I've used it enough to knock Coke bottles off the rock pile three times out of five—from the house!"

He kept his smile, but now it was beginning to look both forced and at the same time malevolent. "Don't you know that's just a .22 target pistol? Maybe you can kill a bird with it, but no more. The slug is only the size of a pebble. It would just . . ." and here he paused ". . . just infuriate a man . . . ."

She kept it leveled at his head.

12

David's ascent was rapid, and as he neared the metal above, he saw a large round aperture into which he floated. He traveled up through this cylinder for perhaps fifty feet, then suddenly found himself inside the spacecraft.

He nearly lost his balance when he took in the sight before him. It was like an entire planet, with rolling mountains, waterfalls which rose vertically, homes and footpaths, with no ceiling overhead but the stars, yet soft, pleasant light everywhere. Around him stood thousands of couples in formations of a hundred each, dressed in splendid, regal clothing, all of different types, and the couples representing hundreds of skin colors and features, each distinct, yet every one strikingly handsome. No one paunchy, skinny, homely nor even balding was here. Such apparently did not exist in matter.

As soon as he was aboard and the shaft below him closed, great forces began accelerating the entire structure out into space . . . and David merely stood there, staring at the great company before him.

Finally, an aged white-haired man with aqua-colored skin, his wife beside him, stepped forward. "You are David," he said, in perfect English. "I am Teca. You are the first of our brother race Aelor has allowed here, and we honor you. And this," he said, motioning to his wife, "is Sherusé."

David's impression of the man changed as he came close and spoke. "Aged" was not properly descriptive of him, for there was none of the crippling or the wrinkles of age. Yet he looked ancient. It detracted not a bit from his attractiveness, nor that of his equally ancient wife. On the contrary, it gave them a maturity beyond his power to comprehend.

"I am honored to be in your presence," he said softly. "We are both followers of Aelor."

The man smiled. "Of course. All that exists is part of him."

David was led past the great ranks of people (heads of state, he surmised), along a wide path toward a large spherical structure looming before him. The three entered and Teca led him to a seat in a wide, brightly decorated area of what was apparently his airborne home.

The ancient one smiled. "You have questions. Go ahead."

"What is this we're traveling on?" David asked immediately. "How is it that there are no sides, no roof?"

"As you have already learned, what you would call force fields operate well for this use—they are quite as effective as metal for the dome of the ship, and they don't block the view. Of course, all the machinery is below us."

"And force fields explain the suspended vertical columns of water?" David asked, looking at a mass of liquid heaped high beside them with no supports, colorful marine creatures swimming through it. "And my language. You got it from Pélu's tapes in the wrecked spaceship?"

"Yes," was Teca's reply. "But you have deeper questions, I'm sure."

David looked squarely at the couple, probing their expressions. They looked kind, but strong and unbending. "What is to be done with me? Am I to stay in your world?"

"No," Teca replied with finality. "It is in the plan of Aelor that you should come here and unveil some of the great drama on earth in which we have great interest. But you cannot stay."

"I will go back to my world?" David asked.

"I do not think so. Your companion who was on Pélu's ship has already been transported into the next dimension. The telora will probably want to take you into their plane. After being here in matter, I doubt you could return to antimatter."

There was a long pause. "Do you mean the telora will kill me?"

The man looked up in surprise. "I don't know what you mean. They would simply transport you to their plane. Your body would become more like theirs."

"Like theirs?"

"No body at all. That is, *we* can't see it. Their bodies are real enough in their dimension, yet so different that they're beyond our perception. You see, the telora need no such elemental things as spaceships or food for body fuel or even sleep. In our lower order of creation, we joy in learning and developing these elementary principles as we help build part of Aelor's ever-expanding universe. But then, finally, we graduate into new bodies, new dimensions not limited by the severe restrictions on these bodies of ours."

"But what," David demanded "do the telora have to do with me? Why can't I meet Aelor himself?"

"No man can meet Aelor, even for an instant, and remain in this dimension. He would be consumed. The telora help us . . . guide us. They are over us, observing all and rejoicing in all —the same as we do with lesser orders like animals on our planets. Itheran himself, the greatest of our telora, will be there to tell what Aelor wishes."

David eased himself back on the soft wall behind him.

"And you," David asked, "what is your role in the worlds of matter?"

Both Teca and his wife smiled benignly. "We were the first. Born after your first ones, after they had followed the Twisted One instead of Aelor."

"And has the Twisted One ever been here to hurt you?"

"No. We have always lived in the flow of Aelor's power. Our universe is what yours could have been—trillions of families scattered to the distant stars, still multiplying happiness, still discovering, still innovating. Your race was confined to antimatter.

"But this is all the telora have told me—and, I think, possibly all they know themselves," Teca concluded. "Now what will you tell us? How, David, did Aelor himself visit your world? And what. . . ."

From this point on, it was Teca who did the questioning and David went on for hours describing Aelor's mission, the rejections, the whole story. The old man's eyes fairly burned with excitement, dismay, disbelief, as he probed deeper and deeper.

After several hours, Teca said at last, "Enough. It is too much to absorb." He stood and looked at his wife, then said slowly, significantly, "It is the grandest, most mystifying truth of all universes, times, and dimensions, part of all that ever does or ever will exist. The telora will greatly desire to look into this. Our telora have never been to antimatter—and I had been told we would hear of antimatter's story before we passed from this plane, Sherusé."

He dismissed David then, and the earthling was shown to

an area near an inset pool. He slumped wearily on the yielding foam-like substance rising beside it. Before long he was asleep.

For the next several days, as they hurtled toward the center of the universe at speeds of multiple million light years an hour, David met and talked to the potentates in their unique homes. Each was leader of at least a million stars' worth of planets, all peopled by his own offspring. All were unique in personality, yet each bore the indelible stamp of being linked to the power, love, and joy that flows from Aelor. David's own knowledge of the Omniscient broadened daily in contact with this second race of humanoids who lived to their full potential in accord with their Creator. It was all Eden here—a gigantic universe of Eden, not of mawkish innocence but true fulfill-men of character in each life.

After five days of spaceflight, the gigantic craft started slowing down and soon settled on a planet. Beyond them, in the direction they were headed, glowed a brilliance wider and deeper than any sun, a sharp, hard light outlining objects as sharply as a knife.

Teca and his wife led David off the craft, and after a ride in a small airborne machine, they came to an undeveloped valley. It was uninhabited except for animals of various sizes and descriptions. Mountains loomed to the sides, bodies of water were etched into the forest line at the valley's edge. It was as lovely a pastoral scene as David had ever observed, on canvas or in real life.

Teca stared at it and murmured, "Here it all began," gripping the hand of his long-time wife.

"Is this the center of the universe?" David asked gently.

The ancient one laughed. "To us it is. We were created by Aelor here. But there"—he pointed at the brightness beyond— "there in that brilliance now uncountable light years away is the making of our worlds, flinging fiery masses of raw material —and all of us exploding from it. Only the telora come from there. This is our closest point."

It seemed impossible that these two people standing with him had only a few thousands years ago been a newly created man and woman with no skills, no mechanical devices, no education, and through their total absorption in the energies of Aelor had peopled a universe and moved to such heights. "And could not your skills enable you to explore the center, too?" David asked. "Surely you can guard against heat some way."

"Perhaps," came the reply. "But it is not the will of Aelor. Only the telora go there."

David looked around. Here, too, was potential temptation. He did not want now to be a part of producing any.

People began to arrive. All those who had been on the spacecraft, and now many more, lined the valley's side in precise rows and columns. The diversity of features, colors, mannerisms, and dress was unlimited. At last the valley was full. Teca, his wife, and David stood at the center. Before them stretched a wide road, perhaps a quarter mile long, which culminated in a plateau slightly above the rest of the valley.

Suddenly, there was a great roar like hurricane winds, and all the people were silent. The sounds increased, and magnificent music began such as David had never heard, engulfing the valley and lifting his spirit.

And then, without their moving at all, David saw something changing form before him. On the plateau was a roaring tempest of fire, and all about him, above each person, were great balls of brilliant, burning light, stacked higher than David could see. As he shielded his eyes and kept looking, he realized these must be the telora, blazes of golden light becoming more and more the forms of men, terrible in their countenances.

The people stood there, obviously excited, but with no expressions of fear whatever. Then Teca and Sherusé began walking toward the plateau where Itheran in his blazing deep-red glory stood waiting for them. And David felt somehow compelled to follow.

He noticed that all the hosts of the telora, standing as if on platforms above their people, were dressed just like those below them. They could assume any form they wished, David surmised, so they made themselves look like the people they helped.

The fear was ebbing out of David now, but when Itheran spoke to Teca and his wife, the strong purpose in his thunderous voice chilled the earthling. He could understand nothing of the conversation going on before him between the couple and the highest of all telora.

The dialogue had all the aura of being a solemn, monu-

(147)

mental ceremony which David could sense was of extreme significance to everyone there. Somehow all were sharing, all were hearing. David kept staring into the face of Itheran, wondering. . . .

Suddenly, as the speech by the magnificent Itheran ended, both the ancient man and the woman before him were consumed in a brilliant essence. David could not tell whether it was flames or heat or what, only that it was light, and that as it appeared, the progenitors of the race became a part of that essence.

David stood there, stunned yet sharing in the joy that was part of the very air. A great shout merged into thunderous singing, and the earthling could only stand with a deep sense of unworthiness.

Finally, Itheran addressed David by thought: "What you have seen is only the walking into a higher world . . . as you must do. But first, we honor your coming here. We are to learn from you of Aelor's conquests in antimatter."

For the next two hours, David felt as if he were detached from his body and simply allowing his mind to flow not only to and from Itheran but throughout the entire company, all absorbing each thought which the telora drew from David, exposing the ugliness of planet Earth and the incomparable epic of the anguish and joy of Aelor-ké. Everything about the human project was of intense interest to all assembled, and apparently David was fulfilling Aelor's plan to unfold portions of the greatest drama to the universe of matter.

Itheran finally stood, motionless and terrible in his silence, his thoughts of awe and near disbelief still coursing through him, through the thousands of great ones of Teca's race, and through their telora. "You have heard . . ." he said simply. "You have heard . . . you understand what it is to us. . . ."

He then looked at David. "No, you will not go to the higher world now. I would have hoped to have given you that joy. But Aelor has decreed that you must go back to your own twisted planet. Marcor, son of Pélu, will take you."

With that, the entire massive army of telora, including Itheran himself, slowly disappeared as if burning away, and the huge formations of Teca's people were left alone in the gentle valley.

A bronze man disengaged himself from the ranks and walked assuredly to the earthling. He was a head taller than David, wide-shouldered, muscular. At first he simply stood there, a touch of a smile on the corners of his mouth, and then his thoughts started flowing into David's.

"We have a long journey together," the bronze man was saying, "and you have much to tell me of my father. We must face, too, the explosion of the quasars, but Aelor will pass us through, and into the void."

On facing the thought of actually leaving matter, of re-entering the Twisted One's domain, David began to desire nothing more than to stay here, no matter how little he belonged. If it weren't for his intense desire to see Charlotte again, he felt he would have begged to be left here, on some small place, even alone where he could do no harm. . . .

But Marcor was filling his brain with questions, and motioning him forward to their readied spacecraft.

13

The first days of their journey back, David answered Marcor's innumerable questions about Pélu, watched historical and contemporary events on the viewer which would pursue at length whatever his mind followed, and dreamed incessantly of Charlotte and what his homecoming would be like.

It was about the ninth day that Marcor, watching the controls, announced, "Antimatter."

"We're close?"

Marcor laughed and walked to a seat. "We're *in* it." Then he turned on the contemporary news channel of the viewer. Nothing. The central communications channel. Nothing.

David sat silently beside him. His anxieties about smashing into the quasars had been drained from him now because of a miracle he didn't even know had happened. And Marcor had without hesitation flown through them, never questioning that Aelor would change the normal patterns of events to let them pass.

Marcor was smiling at him, reading his thoughts. "It is good," he said, "that I am to leave antimatter after putting you home. It would not be well for me to start thinking the way you do."

About three days into the void of antimatter, David felt the first touches of his sickness: a sore throat. Soon his body weakened, and fever began to control it. Marcor was at a loss to understand, but he attentively swabbed his forehead and tried to feed him.

Perspiration soaked his clothing; his mind swirled with a thousand inanities; aches in his neck, throat and back combined with the fever. It continued on and on, with David's mind keeping no track of anything but the phantasms in his thoughts, oblivious to their travel—until the change occurred.

The violence of a sudden shift in the spacecraft sent both David and Marcor sprawling into the control area. An immediate shaking began, fast and vicious as if a giant dog were shaking a snake. Marcor had lunged at the control panels and, holding on to a bar with one hand, was twisting, pulling and shoving knobs and buttons.

Yet the shaking continued, steadily violent to the degree that neither man could even communicate to the other. Warning lights and sounds pled for attention all over the control panel, yet Marcor's lunging and adjusting did nothing. The craft was inexorably being drawn off course, and power thrusts to right it created such violent shaking that he feared it would break apart. Moment after moment the craft accelerated in its new direction. Finally, as David felt himself being shaken into unconsciousness, he felt Marcor's arms about him, saw his hand push a panel, then felt himself being catapulted with Marcor from the craft into the speckled blackness.

*   *   *

David regained consciousness almost immediately as they fell through space, both of them locked into a protective force field, their craft no longer in sight. For what seemed an interminable time, they hurtled into increasingly dense, hot vapors until they abruptly smashed through a thick substance, after which they tumbled for miles down an obscure surface until they hit a solid wall of grayness which knocked David unconscious.

He awoke painfully to a strange sensation. About eight men, hairy and thick-bodied with dull burlap-like materials around their waists, were lifting him and Marcor by the use of poles. The force field kept the men four feet away, so that they were being carried as if encased in a block of ice.

Jostled, bewildered, trying to communicate with Marcor but getting no meaningful answers, he sat on his floor of force a foot above gray, vaporous obscurity and tried to see something recognizable.

He saw nothing but the gray wall and horizon until the men turned into an opening in the wall. Now everything was still gray, but tiny lanes with compartments like rabbit hutches ran haphazardly in all directions. It was primitive. In each cell-like compartment, tall sticks sharpened at the top imprisoned whatever was within. David caught glimpses of animals and men staring dull-eyed, fearful, angry.

Finally, they were dropped unceremoniously before a bull-like little man with red, unkempt hair, a gouged face, and badly scarred legs. Behind him, in a half-dozen compartments, several men and some dogs and pigs were in various positions and conditions on what looked like hospital equipment. Fires flickered. David caught the eyes—and the terror—of one of the men, whose foot was opened to the bone.

The man with the gouged face ordered torches applied to the force field, then gigantic smashing equipment, and finally explosive devices right atop David and Marcor's heads—but nothing would break the field. His malevolent gestures demanded they emerge, yet it was he who seemed nervous, fearful of something.

Suddenly Marcor, who had been standing and watching it all, walked out unconcernedly. A dozen men were immediately upon him, throwing him to the ground. After binding his hands, they yanked him to his feet and began interrogation.

Marcor made no sound, his magnificent bronze body rest-

(151)

ing easy on the balls of his feet, a smile playing at the corners of his mouth. They struck him with clenched fists across the jaw, but still he stood there smiling. Other blows fazed him no more. When the men began to twist his arms cruelly and still no pain crossed the bronze man's eyes, the gouge-faced gnome yelled at the men to stop, then stared at Marcor for a long time. Finally, he pushed him back into the force field.

The two of them were then carried, in the same manner as before, into a large cube of glassy metal, much unlike the rest of this gray world.

They stood there, encased, but in a moment the compartment's metal floor disappeared beneath them and they fell, accelerating downward. Then their direction was slowly reversed, as if they were being dropped into a giant slingshot, and finally they were hurtling up through the atmosphere, smashing through a thick obstacle and out into the heavy vapors.

Their propulsion was of decidedly greater force than a giant slingshot, for they continued acceleration for quite some time, but finally were carried by momentum alone.

"What in the world?" David was asking of Marcor, as they rushed through vapors, still protected by the force field.

The man from matter was shaking his head as he had seen David do. "I have no more idea than you. Who they are or where we are at this instant, I do not know. The people there were mystified by the force field, but I didn't understand their other concepts. As soon as the leader understood I felt no pain his thought was, 'How did this one get here? We must launch him to the—' " Here Marcor paused, bracing himself against a corner of the force field to keep his balance. "The thought was 'original entry bag,' that is, an island-size bag, a hollow spheroid, and apparently much like the gray world we just left."

Though the thickness of the vapors and fumes distorted their view, occasionally they would pass close by a huge mass which looked like a flat wall yet indeed could have been the skin of a gigantic bag. And eventually they did smash dead center into one of these, and on through.

They tumbled out into a world of sparkling light and green and blue colors.

David looked around. A meadow! They were in a meadow, with great leafy trees drooping with ripe fruit, thick green grass, and a rippling creek edged by more fruit trees. Green countryside extended as far as they could see. The skin above was a delightful blue, light was a steady sparkling from everywhere, and little tropic-colored birds sang and flew by them.

"What in the world?" David said again, standing stiffly.

"*The* world? Certainly not *your* world," Marcor commented, using his pocket computer to release the force field around them. They walked to the stream, picked huge apples, pears and peaches. They drank from the stream, ate the fruit, and rested.

Some yards away, they noticed, a man was seated on the creek bank, eating. As they positioned themselves so they could see up and down the stream, they realized there were numerous men and women eating or strangely contorting their bodies. They looked like earth people of various races.

To their left some distance away, a white man in American-style clothing sat languidly eating peaches, and David walked toward him. As he got closer, he noticed that hundreds of peach pits were scattered around him.

"Do you speak English?"

"Of course," the eater said, without looking up, continuing his feast.

"Uh, we're new here," David began again.

"Isn't everybody?" The man lazily rose, and David noticed his leg was gashed and his jawbone at an odd angle, as if it had been broken. "Have any candies or cakes with you?" the eater asked. "Say, *he's* a bit different!" he added, nodding at Marcor. "Do you suppose there really *was* life on other planets?" The question was put absently, and the eater's mind was back on the peaches.

Marcor produced several wafers and handed them to the man, indicating he should eat.

"Mmmmm!" the man grunted, "haven't had chocolate like that before! How 'bout more?" His eyes were dull, lifeless. To David he seemed heavy, obese. Yet he was slender.

Marcor handed him more wafers and started plying him with questions. But the eater knew nothing of where he was, only that they were amidst food and meadows and blueness above, and that if they had questions they should go back to "the Receiver."

"Who's he?" David asked.

"Now, look, don't get smart! You got the same speeches from him that I did. How much more of that chocolate you got?" the man asked Marcor, reaching for another.

"Unlimited," Marcor replied, his fingers on his small black computer. "How many can you eat?"

"Unlimited."

"Excellent," Marcor rejoined. "Take us to 'the Receiver,' and we will keep the supply steady."

They began walking, with the eater silently leading the way. He caught David staring at the ugly gash above his knee. "Oh, it won't take long—it'll happen to *you* soon enough."

"A gashed leg?" David asked. "How?"

The man laughed maliciously and long, then with taunting tones said, "It is *you* who will gash it. You—yes, you yourself!" He began laughing again, almost controlled by it, then finally added, "Only three weeks . . . that's all I've been here . . . bodies don't last long, not long at all!"

And with that he was silent again, even morose as he continued to lead them.

Finally, they reached the top of a small hill overlooking a pleasant valley. The eater pointed out a simplistic structure in its center, with an Oriental seated on a dais before it. He was talking to another like himself. As they stared at the scene, the eater grabbed for the computer, at the same time smashing at Marcor's head with a rock. Leaping away, he began running. Marcor, though stunned, was quickly after him, and in great, flying leaps soon had reached him, knocked him to the ground, and retrieved his precious computer. He then gave the man more chocolates and motioned him away.

Whether he left or not, David was not sure, for Marcor quickly set up a focus on the center of the valley which brought the men and their voices TV-screen close. They were Oriental, and David could understand nothing of their conversation. They watched the situation on the image before them for a long time, and finally the one Oriental bowed to the other and moved off.

Then, at the spot where he had been sitting, a cart rolled up with the body of a man on it. The body, when it was before the Receiver, suddenly took life, rose and began talking to the him. The conversation was again in language unintelligible to David. The Receiver, weirdly enough, had metamorphosed into a person of the same culture as the new arrival—dark reddish skin, high cheek bones, flowing robes.

Their conversation lasted quite long, but finally the man bowed to the Receiver and he, too, moved off.

The procedure then repeated itself. Another cart rolled up, but this time the body on it was that of a white man. It took life and rose trembling to face the Receiver, whose appearance had now metamorphosed from Indian to white man. This time David could understand the conversation.

"Well, yes," the new arrival was saying, "it really is a very nice body. I mean, I don't want to cause trouble or anything. It's just that I can't understand why we had to wait *so* long. I mean with *nothing*—just nothingness in those crazy lines of nothings, not knowing what terrible things might be ahead. You know: months of anxieties, not knowing, wondering, with nothing to communicate with to other nothings. After all, I was killed *years* ago!"

The Receiver, looking ruggedly handsome and about 35, smiled expansively. "But we've been under terrible pressure you know. It's not easy to make the *quality* bodies we insist on here. Let's forget all the delays now and—"

"But I thought here it was done with a snap of the fingers! Omnipotence and all that!"

The Receiver's face clouded. "Not quite: only old Spoilsport has that."

The new arrival blanched and sat down. "You mean—"

"Oh, I assure you it's much more fun down here. A veritable delight, in fact."

"But God—"

"Simply '*He*' will suffice, if you don't mind," the other interrupted irritably. "No, you didn't make it in *His* direction. And I warn you that you would do well not to talk of that.

"Now, to get on with it, let me explain about your body. As I said, it's far superior to any model old Spoilsport ever dreamed up, and you'll be delighted with it, I'm sure. Its features include:

(155)

"Number one. No pain whatever: messages of danger to the body are simply relayed to the brain for appropriate action.

"Two. Full development of every pleasure sense. Taste buds of acute and exquisite quality cover all areas of the mouth and lips and throat. The stomach is designed to handle unlimited supplies of food, simply passing off excess beyond calorie need. Also, large areas of the arms have hidden taste buds so that you can rub food on them and get quite the same effect. At least 50 percent of your body is highly erotic so that the most intense pleasures can be sustained. Retinal tissue, etc., has been distributed in dozens of areas for additional pleasures of sight."

The new arrival was rubbing a piece of fruit on his arm and smiling. "Just like I'm really tasting it," he said.

"You are—those are genuine taste buds!"

"And sex is just as real?"

"Oh, quite!"

"The Playboy Philosophy realized!" the new arrival offered cheerfully, starting to catch the spirit of it all.

"Yes, but here it's never subject to the law of diminishing pleasures. On earth it becomes a drag. Here the pleasure always remains as intense. You see, Spoilsport is quite an accurate appellation for that other maker of bodies. He *could* have made it so pleasures never diminished."

"Well, how did *you*? I thought you couldn't create."

The Receiver's face darkened again. "Let's get one thing straight. I run things here, but I'm not in charge of *everything* here, you know. You've heard about the one who is." His face darkened further. "And, no, we can't *create* bodies, but we can use raw materials and processes. I want you to know that your body, made with ingrafting of animal materials, molecular reconstructions, and a thousand processes you wouldn't have any idea about, took millions of work hours. Of course, we have plenty of cheap help. But remember—millions of hours just for *your* body. This is back to the original Eden model—*plus*. So appreciate it!"

The Receiver was smiling, hard lines etched on his face, obviously enjoying his role, his eyes hungrily following every naïve expression of the newcomer.

"Then this *is* Utopia?" the other asked, smiling back awkwardly.

"In its own unique way, of course," the Receiver responded. "Now you're simply to walk out there and enjoy yourself—any way you wish."

"Uh," the other looked at him nervously, suspiciously. "And in this Utopia, there's no lying?"

"Of course, there is," the Receiver replied. "That's all up to you . . . but I assure you that I have told you nothing but facts. Now, be careful. Remember—that's the only body you've got, so keep it tidy . . . and run along now. . . ."

As the man turned to walk off, the Receiver started to laugh, slowly at first, and then uproariously, a gigantic smirk on his face. The man turned around, watching him as he laughed even harder. "Ah, the delights that are here," the Receiver exclaimed, walking over to the man and rubbing a banana on his arm. "Here, rub it, eat, look, laugh! Yes, laugh, laugh with me! Laugh with me!"

The other obviously was not as filled with mirth but attempted a good laugh, and as he turned again to go, the Receiver walloped a huge gong which nearly startled the man into falling. "See," the Receiver gloated, "no pain. On earth the sound would have given you a terrible headache. Yet you are still warned of danger. What happiness!"

As David and Marcor were watching closely, trying to understand, a voice from behind them suddenly cut their viewing short. "How are you doing that—projecting that image?" it demanded.

They turned to see a thin, refined-looking man in a natty suit. But it was ripped in several places, his face had an angry, large bruise on one side, and his right arm and chest had been gored or smashed somehow. Distraught anger controlled his face and body.

"How are you doing that?" he demanded again. "Do you have weapons? We've got to *kill* that sadist; we've just *got* to!"

David stared at the man, and finally asked, "Who did this to you—the wounds?"

The man sneered. "*He* did, you fool. And *I* did, just as *you* will before long. Have you been here so short a time you don't understand *anything!* Not even what the absence of pain *does* to you!" he fairly screamed. The man grabbed David and shook him. "Do you have weapons?"

He was looking at them with angry, festering eyes and finally backed off. David asked, "But why?"

The mangled man gave a gesture of despair. "You're still believing it! Don't you know what's inside you? Don't you know you'll quickly despise the pleasures even as you gulp them? Can't you see you'll want to hurt and kill because it's part of you? You'll take from others even though you have. You'll feed upon your pleasures like your vomit, no purpose, just gulping pleasures as your thoughts run to a million more pleasures, to climbing above the others and taking from them . . . to *be* somebody. Good God, we can't be just animals sucking up things to tickle the sensors they've sewn into these hellion bodies!" he screamed.

David backed away from the man as he advanced with a heavy stick. "But you can't attack those who made them. They'll do *worse* than kill you."

"You think I don't know that! You think I don't know about the places they have to torment every one of your senses with foods and sights you can have no part of?"

David was standing close to Marcor now, edging back. "But if they love to torment, why don't they just put everyone on spits and roast them or whatever they're supposed to do?"

"Fool! Damned double fool! Don't you even know yet the terror of being caught? Don't you know that they feed upon the anxieties, that terror is delicious to them like aroma on a steak? Now—*what weapons do you have!*" he shouted, throwing himself at David, who yelled that he had none whatever.

The crazed man grabbed the heavy stick and stood up, screaming at the Receiver, then ran down toward him.

The Receiver simply smiled, and looked up casually as the enraged man descended toward him. His serenity was unbroken until very suddenly he realized that someone was reading his mind, that someone was up on the hill from which this man was coming, that someone was monitoring his actions. More quickly than David could comprehend, the atmosphere was charged with thundering, enraged hurricane-force winds, and great bolts of black lightning shot from the Receiver directly at him and Marcor.

But Marcor had thrown up a force field about them, and was at the same time slicing the ground from beneath them so that they dropped through the skin of the hollow spheroid and were quickly falling through grey, vaporous space again.

* * *

They fell for hours, doing everything possible to avoid the bags, which David began to see were of all sizes, some so small that only a few creatures could be within—if any were.

But at one point they found themselves heading directly into something that must have been as large as England. Gray and rugged, it took up their entire vision, and when they smashed into it, the crust was so thick they were stopped somewhere within. As they stood buried in the blackness, Marcor used his force field to slice away the rocky substance above them, and then they climbed to air above.

The experience of climbing out was much like emerging from a manhole in Harlem. They pulled themselves through the round hole near the gutter in a dirty, narrow street. Old brick buildings, some with blistering paint, some blackened, all festooned with rusted railings, old wooden steps, ugly windows, and ill-dressed people sitting on steps or staring out windows, completed the picture of a rundown inner city.

They looked for a while and then began walking, watching the people who looked with distrust at the newcomers. All their faces were white. All were shabbily dressed.

For at least ten blocks they walked, past uninviting stores, abandoned service stations, gutted old buildings now unused. A boy about eight sitting on a bottom step which leaned out into the street stared at them. Marcor went over to him and smiled, then handed him some chocolate.

The boy accepted it, ate it, held out his hand for more, all the while keeping his eyes on the strangers. Marcor was obviously reading his mind, and asked him questions about where they were. The boy answered nothing.

As they walked on, he followed them. No matter what they said to the boy, or what Marcor thought to him, he stayed behind, holding out his hand for more food. Marcor finally handed him a sackful of fruits.

After they had crossed a bridge, the buildings became decidedly better, and the faces distinctly non-white. They looked Mexican to David, or Latins of various origins.

With the boy trailing them, they walked on. People here seemed even more unfriendly, glaring at the white and bronze skins with distrust. Fear began creeping up David's throat.

After about a half hour of walking through this residential and small-business area which was well kept yet relatively poor, they emerged into a community much like it except that the people all looked Oriental. The lines of racial demarcation were abrupt—one street to another, with no mixture in either. But they all had in common great piles of rubble, and crumbling blackened walls, whole blocks which looked like bomb damage. And once during their walk they did hear great explosions in the distance.

Finally, they came to the suburbs of the little city. The first blocks were populated by more Orientals, and then they entered the really plush areas with huge lawns and parks, well-swept sidewalks, and rambling newly painted houses. Here, all the faces were black. The only exception was the presence of a few clean but servant-dressed whites raking leaves or washing cars or scrubbing the walls of the spacious homes.

They walked slowly here, drinking it all in. Once they saw men in military uniforms racing up a street, but they walked the other way and evaded them.

They soon came to a large park, where in the center a group of men were gathered around a thick willow tree. Walking through the new-mown grass, David and Marcor headed toward them, the little white boy trailing behind, his third sack of food in his hand.

As they drew closer, they saw the group was composed of six well-dressed Negroes who had a white man up against the tree, a thick, heavy chain around his chest. The chain cut into him so deeply David thought he must be dead. But he was not, and the chain as it was tightened a bit more evoked groans from the white man, who lived in a body obviously capable of feeling pain. The black men watched, taunting, intent on their victim and oblivious to the approach of the others.

"Detach the chain!" Marcor commanded.

The Negroes, startled, immediately reached into shoulder

holsters for their pistols, but relief spread across their faces as they saw their unarmed adversaries. "What's it to you, whitey-lover?" a big, beefy man twisting the chain asked. "Looks like you've got some white blood in you yourself. We've got chain enough for all three of you."

"Let him go!" Marcor commanded again.

One man pointed his pistol directly at the bronze man, who was adjusting dials on his black box. When the Negro fired, only a small spat was heard because of a silencer attachment. The bullet ricocheted off Marcor's chest.

The men gaped. Several more fired at Marcor, and finally they all threw themselves upon him and David. But as they hit, the force of their own impact against the force field crumpled them as if they had tackled stone walls. David picked up one of the fallen guns, pointed it at the men and ordered them to run—and quickly.

Marcor leaped to release the white man, who slumped onto the green grass, then slowly looked up at his rescuers.

He said nothing. For a long time he only stared. There was anguish in his eyes.

Then the rescued white painfully walked to retrieve a gun, nearly hidden by a root, and began to walk off. But as he did so, he surreptitiously aimed the pistol as casually as he would have a camera right at the head of the little boy. Then he pulled the trigger. Blood spouted from his head, like red water from a hose. After watching the boy fall, he pulled the sack of food out of his lifeless hand and walked off unconcernedly.

David stood staring in disbelief. Outraged, he ran and leaped upon the man, hacking at the hand which held the gun, finally getting the weapon into his own hands.

"You murdered that little boy!" He stood glaring at him, seething. David forced the killer over to the tree and made him sit with his back against its huge trunk.

The man was glaring back at him, not in the least cowed. "What kind of stupid remark is that? He was just as old as you are. You think he was *born* in that body or something? And who do you think *you* are—some great white knight out rescuing maidens? You got your guns out of the deal."

"You mean," David asked, still unable to control his voice, "that this is the way you reward our kindness when—"

The man gave a loud, laughing snort. "Kindness! What would any of us know about it now? The *kindness* has all been stripped off every one of us, like fat from bacon!"

Marcor had been watching quietly and interrupted with: "You mean because the source of kindness is not here?"

The man did not answer. He simply rose and began walking away, baleful eyes on the two men. David demanded, "You can't walk off like that. We'll have the cops here so fast—"

At that the man stopped, turned around and began laughing again. "What? The Nazi Storm troopers? The SS? Sure, we have cops, just like we have doctors and hospitals to fix my broken ribs."

They let him walk away. Marcor and David looked at each other, and after a time they sat down by the tree, stretching their legs out on the clipped, bright-green grass. They noticed an ebony-black Negro who emerged from the front door of a big split-level home across the street, walked past the car in his driveway (almost a Mercury Cougar style), and advanced toward the strangers. His suit was of very high quality, his carriage genteel, and when he finally reached them, his speaking was equally cultured.

"Come into my home, gentlemen. You are obviously new here. I believe in taking good care of our whites, and I deplore this violence. Come . . . ."

They followed him through the park and across the street to his home. Inside, they were led to a large, carpeted living room, with oil paintings on the wall and Early American furniture. As the black host motioned for them to be seated, he signalled in a voice that would carry into other rooms, "Boy!"

A white man, perhaps in his fifties and dressed in a red uniform, appeared in response. "Bring us some sandwiches and drinks," the servant was instructed. "And be sure to get them cold this time."

A beautiful Negro woman entered the room, and the host went to kiss her, then introduced her to them as his wife.

David began to hope this might be an oasis of at least some normalcy in this society, but Marcor began asking questions like, "Why do you feel the whites are so inferior?"

"Oh, not all of them are. The ghettos are the real problems. If they could have good jobs like we give them out

(162)

here, they could live well. Like Mary here." The Negro motioned to a young white girl, rather fat and pimply, sitting in a corner sewing. "She's got it made and is happy as a lark."

"That is what your words are saying," Marcor said, "but not what your brain is thinking. You hate us. You fear many, many things . . . and that is why you have us here, so you can get my black box and know its secrets and its power."

The man smiled. "Of course. It takes little to figure that out. And you probably noticed one of our fears in the form of soldiers tromping around out there."

He was motioning to the large picture window through which David could see men across the street in uniforms. They looked much the same as those they had evaded before. A squad of six, they were interrogating a white man with a rake in his hands, who was standing in front of a blue two-story house. David stared at them, and when his host handed him binoculars, he saw a weird anachronism. The soldiers were Indonesian-looking, yet their uniforms were distinctly Nazi, complete with swastika armbands.

"Our fears are your fears," the homeowner said to the newcomers. "They propagate that they are, of course, the 'master race,' using a history lesson to build a power machine. They even have a mustached Führer, but he's hardly Aryan." As the man was speaking, he was also following with a scope atop a .30-.30 rifle two of the neo-Nazis mounting the steps of the home across the street. As they began knocking, he shot them one after the other in the heads, with only muffled spats being heard in the living room. Almost simultaneously all four of the remaining Nazis flopped to the ground, bullets from other directions having killed them.

Their host replaced his weapon in its cabinet and peered out the rifle slot in the window. "We're very well organized here. The fact is, Nazis seldom come. We're too well armed, but they know they must try. And their power is growing."

"Yet," Marcor said to him, "the spirit ruler of this particular spheroid likes many different factions of power. You don't have to worry about their taking over completely."

"You must have been reading my mind," the black man said.

"How else would I have known?" Marcor asked. "You know I'm a newcomer."

The black man's grin disappeared. His jaw snapped shut.

"Yes," Marcor continued, "I see some things . . . such as how white you yourself were when you lived on Earth in a land called Rhodesia and used natives to entertain you . . . and how your wife lived in a land called Peru. And how—" here he turned to the chubby white girl sewing—"how you, young lady, were once golden brown, and poor, but very beautiful and very much desired."

The black man sat, cringing. David thought by his expression that he would grab a weapon for protection, but he didn't move his hands.

"No," Marcor explained, "I am not one of the Terrible Ones your thoughts are dwelling on. In fact, we will leave now."

"No!"

Marcor was leading David out the door, then onto the lawn, his computer tight in his hand. "No," the homeowner was insisting, with terror in his voice. "Take me with you."

"We are leaving this spheroid."

"They'll kill me! They saw me take you in! My neighbors will never—" he was screaming as they forced the grass and dirt apart and slid through the thick skin of the giant bag to the vapors beyond.

*　　*　　*

Though they tried not to, after some time Marcor and David found themselves once more escaping the oppressive vapors by crashing into another gray mass. They burst through the skin but this time did not tumble onto a hard surface. Instead, they felt their bodies sloshing through a lake of thick yet airy material. As they came to a halt, they sank to the bottom, and were a dozen feet below the surface of the whipped-meringue-like substance.

They adjusted the force field so that they could maneuver and walked along the bottom. Eventually their heads emerged above the stuff, and they saw before them a large island, with giant tropical vegetation crowding every inch. They had to grasp thick, long leaves to pull themselves onto the forest floor.

Slithering around, under and through the thick foliage, during the next quarter hour they twice heard roarings and screams so blood-chilling that David had visions of a prehistoric *Tyrannosaurus rex* ripping his prey. Yet, for all the sounds around them, when danger did come they did not hear its stealthy approach. Marcor had not an instant's warning in which to throw up his force fields when heavy clubs rained down upon them from trees above. Both fell unconscious into the thick bed of moist vegetation.

They awoke to see two hairy bipeds, holding clubs in Neanderthal fashion. Indeed, their commands to their captives were no more than grunts and growls, and they looked, David thought, like refugees from a museum display.

Tough vines held the captives' hands securely behind their backs, and David was suddenly aware that the creatures had stripped them of their clothing. He looked over at Marcor, then at the clothes held by the hairy apparitions. Even the box was in their possession.

The two captives were shoved roughly through the slapping, binding foliage, kicked when they fell until they could brace themselves somehow with their bound hands and rise, and were regularly growled at for more haste. David's head was throbbing painfully from the initial blow, and other bruises were beginning to appear on his body.

The foliage began thinning and finally disappeared behind them. Before them loomed a high, soft mountain which seemed to be bleeding down to the thick yet airy sea. They then came to a crude village of small huts made of dried leaves. As they were being forced to the center of the village, its savage inhabitants emerged from huts, ran past dead animals hanging on poles, past smoldering fires on rocks, to yell at and taunt the bound men, and to throw rocks and sticks. The crowd grew to perhaps fifty, a great press of smelly, hairy bodies. Soon they were standing in the village center, being surveyed by a huge Neanderthal type seated on a large slab of wood, with as regal an expression as his species could conjure up.

Whatever the ritual that followed was, it concluded in a moment: the seated potentate, after throwing dust upon Marcor and David, spat upon them, and they were hustled off to a hut and thrown into the blackness within.

After their eyes adjusted to the lack of light, they saw that this was a large hut and that there were other captives lying tied in various positions around the walls. They all, it became apparent, looked much like their captors in terms of pre-historic hairiness and appearance. Yet they were different in that some were darker and blunter-faced, others thicker and shorter. In the hours they sat in the darkness, thinking and plotting, the only sounds Marcor and David heard were grunts and various unintelligible sounds.

Across from them, a beefy ape-like creature sat glaring directly at them, his eyes red and moving rapidly.

"Hello there, friend," David said. "Some predicament, eh?"

Only a grunt returned his query, and David was becoming convinced that any form of communication would be impossible when a voice beside him, not Marcor's, observed very casually, "Pity about that poor fellow. Understand he was an articulate educator once. But—you know how it is here . . . a body's a body. . . ."

David squinted to make out the speaker. Beside him, if his eyes were right, sat a man like the others: strictly Neanderthal, unshaven, barbarian, looking as if he'd never uttered more than a grunt in his life.

"That's the irony of it," the man was saying. "You have no idea how retarded *I* was—I mean, literally—and what an absolute failure. Guess that's why I like to talk about it . . . in four languages, no less."

David stared in the dull light at the man, trying to see his face, to make sure it was indeed like the others. "But," he asked the dark form, "did you not retain your first intelligence? Did not he? Otherwise, what is a spirit if it doesn't retain thoughts?"

No answer came from the man, and David feared he had said something wrong. But finally the other remarked cuttingly, "You will know soon—if it is true you are actually asking the question."

David's throat and stomach leaped, and he demanded, "What will they do to us? Is there not some way to—"

"None at all that I know of. You, I am sure, as newcomers, were given the chance to bow down and grovel a bit at the proper instant during the ritual and thereby join the tribe."

"But how were we to know that?"

"You weren't. That's the name of the game. So you're to be executed quite spectacularly, along with the rest of us." The man in the shadows said it as if he enjoyed informing David of his fate.

"And why you?"

"The old thing—tribal warfare. They have a very unkind designation for us—slopeheads. They also," he explained, nodding his head at some short, squatty men in the corner, "detest the 'animals.' And, of course, so do we."

They sat in silence for some time, until finally the man spoke again. "I forgot to tell you. There is one chance you have: break out of here, kill the chief and all his bodyguards, and you'll have won their respect enough not to execute you."

"Thanks a lot."

Marcor asked, to get the man's brain thinking along the most informative line, "What happens to you, after the execution?"

His face contorted, and he glared at Marcor.

"I am not taunting," Marcor explained. "I sincerely want to know. You see, we really are newcomers."

The man's jaw dropped. "You mean your body feels no pain?"

Marcor hesitated, then nodded his assent and asked, "But what happens after we leave these bodies?"

The hairy one laughed—a vicious, gloating laugh—and explained, "There is only one thing sure. They start you in the best situation you'll ever know down here, and then it always gets worse. *Always.* You'll become a searcher for a body. Any kind of a body. Even the body and brain of an animal. Men will hunt you down, or other animals will. You'll live in the forest wetness and sleep with it, and yearn for your intelligence —that is, if you can get any body at all."

As the man talked, David thought of Jesus' sending the demons into the herd of pigs. Could it *really* be that men would be driven to this?

"And don't you know," the other was asking, "that when you're asleep the body hunters could come in and possess yours? Or how, as you claw your way out of one of these detestable bags, you have little chance of making it alive to the next? Yet you must always leave eventually. And even if you get to another bag, and claw into its crust, you may end up entombed there, unable to break through."

"But," David asked, "why are these tribesmen going to execute us? Why don't they use our bodies instead of destroying them if they're so valuable?"

He gave another raucus laugh. "And lose the joy of killing you? What could they possibly care about saving a body for anyone else but themselves? Who's going to set up a body clinic here?"

David shook his head as if to drown out the absurdities . . . the viciousness. Had these people really been that evil when they were back on earth? Or had years of being totally separated from Aelor warped them so? Were the fallen angels totally demonic when they first fell? Or were they, too, increasingly twisted?

"Actually," David said aloud, "Earth is quite like hell. But it has the salt of God at work. And hell is like earth, but without traces of God."

Though he waited a long while, he got no answer to his musings. But the man did taunt on by saying, "Just know this: there are a thousand more places, and they'll all be just a bit more terrible and brutalizing, no matter how high the sophistication. Military force and bombs—you know who first thought them up, and certainly he would use them in his exclusive domain. You always keep going down, down, down until you hit the very center of it all, that horrible inferno where they delight in the indescribable. We all know it, and we live in the dread of it. And *they* taste our dread and enjoy it. We hate them for that—and they enjoy even *that* emotion of ours! All is despair, for even those horrors at the lowest level will only finally release us to a new series of who knows what."

"How do you know?" Marcor asked, his eyes boring into the man.

The hairy articulator stared back, pursing his greasy lips.

"How does one get to this center?" Marcor asked.

He gave no answer, but Marcor steadily looked into his eyes, then turned away and settled back against the hut wall.

David slept little that night, tied painfully as he was. None of the other captives seemed to either—except Marcor, who was relaxed.

In the morning they were roughly hustled out to a soft, unvegetated plain far beyond the village. In the center, a circular, house-sized mound of rough rock rose above a ditch which had been dug all around it. At the center of the high mound was a large, black, metal idol protruding from the ground. In the ditch below stood the tribespeople, only their shoulders and heads above ground level. All of them were doing obeisance to the idol. Except the chief. Beside him lay a crate, the only mark of civilization David had seen here.

Without ceremony, the chief pointed to a thick, squatty captive. He was carried and shoved to the idol, then left there, his hands fastened to it.

The chief reached into the crate and pulled out something. David twisted to see what it was, and when he caught sight of it, his mind could hardly accept it. A hand grenade! The chief casually pulled the pin and waited not even a second to toss the gridded death apple up to the captive. It rolled innocently to within a few yards of the man. David found himself ducking with the others, waiting for the explosion.

It came, with lethal consequences.

In the next five minutes, they executed three more of the "animals" in the same manner, one by one.

The fear in David's chest was terrible when the chief walked toward Marcor. He held his hatchet-like weapon in his hand, extending its handle to the bronze man, whose eyes were drilling steadily into the chief's. They stood staring at each other for a few moments; then Marcor, hands tied behind his back, raised his knee and pushed the handle aside.

The chief returned to his crate and commanded more executions, this time including the conversationalist of the night before. As the slaughter continued, Marcor thought into David's mind what the chief's thoughts had been as he offered the weapon. If he had knelt, and then used the weapon to execute another captive, he could have become a part of the tribe, and live.

The chief stepped toward David. He realized the terrible decision before him, and his agony became greater than the single-thrusted fear of the moment before.

The handle was extended to him.

David's thoughts were not fully rational: *the men were to die anyway . . . he could escape later. . . .* But it was primarily fear which almost physically drove him to his knees and then made him, after they untied him, accept the hatchet into his hands. Then he was led over to the crate, and struck hard across the mouth.

He stood there, hatchet in hand, waiting, not daring to look at Marcor.

A new thought alarmed him. It would be *Marcor* they would bring for him to kill. They would test his loyalty to see if he would kill his companion. And as he stood there with his hatchet in hand, with the thought of their bringing Marcor for him to slay, he saw himself a natural part of all this. The agony of his soul in contemplating how much of *himself* was still barbarian drenched him with hatred for the evil within him.

But they did not lead Marcor to the top of the hill. In that David was mistaken, for such a thing as loyalty and friendship had not crossed their minds. It was a "slopehead" they led and tied up there, and the chief gave David a rough shove in his direction.

Even as he stumbled forward, David thought of killing the man up there, of his becoming part of this tribe, of watching Marcor die, of being alone—and without even a conscious plan, he let himself stumble onto the crate, and then grabbed a grenade, and pulling the pin, held it high.

The hairy barbarians dove for cover, and David threw the live grenade into the far side of the ditch, at the same time grabbing another and screaming for Marcor to join him. He threw grenade after grenade into the far ditch, at the same time threatening the others with them. Finally, after more than a dozen had been thrown into the same spot in the ditch, he held onto Marcor, and ran for it, leaping into the depth of the blasted dirt.

Clubs were flying at them now, and as they hit the rocky bottom of the blasted crater, David's heart sank. He stomped and clawed, but nothing happened. Then, suddenly, they broke through, crashing out into the vapors beyond, David holding tightly to Marcor, whose hands were still tightly se-

(170)

cured behind him. Only seconds after their fall, they heard explosions directly behind them, as if grenades were being thrown at their exiting bodies.

This time in the vapors it was completely different. There was no force field to protect them from the terrible heat and suffocating steams. They twisted and tossed, around and down, with David trying desperately both to hold on to Marcor and to get his hands free at the same time. It took hours of grappling, near separation from each other, with muscles shaking and clumsy, before David was able to free him.

Then Marcor held him, and they continued to fall, twisting and turning in the thick atmosphere, perspiring, hardly able to breathe. Again and again they arched their bodies to avoid hitting one of the gray skins which were becoming more numerous. Marcor had clearly in his mind that he wanted to descend to the very pit of this—for what reason David could not fathom. But he apparently had some purpose.

The heat became more and more intense. And then, as the air became so hot that it was nearly impossible to breathe, they were slowly enveloped in tangible blackness. Their falling steadily slowed until they were completely stopped.

They stood in the darkness, feeling, straining for vision, unable to perceive anything of their surroundings. They were up to their waists in a clinging, dry substance, but this was the only tangible thing they could feel. They struggled to walk, and after several hours of inch-by-inch progress, they finally felt something more solid under their feet, and were able to escape the ensnaring substance.

It was some time before they saw any light. Their first glimpse was a faint amber flickering. As they headed to it, they realized it was coming from below. Edging closer and closer, they realized almost too late that all the light was coming from a broken area of the substance on which they were walking. They inched their way on their stomachs to the edge, and looked down. Far, far below them they could see blackness contrasted with leaping flames and dull glows.

They could also now see their immediate surroundings: they were in a cavern of sorts. At least, they could make out the walls, and see that the floor continued again about five feet beyond this fissure.

For a very long time they stared down into the abyss. David fell asleep from exhaustion. When he awoke, Marcor stood, stepped back a bit, and leaped across to the other side of the crevice in the cavern floor. Then he motioned David to leap across.

What if the floor gives way with both our weights there? he thought to the bronze man. *And where can we possibly go?*

But Marcor bade him come. David leaped, and the opposite ledge held.

They continued along the corridors, feeling along the walls, anxiously testing the floor ahead with their feet. Several times they came to holes in it, smaller ones. It seemed, as they peered down, that they were descending closer to the flames below.

Several times they heard voices. Rough, irritated, snarling voices.

Then, as they were in total blackness, the voices came closer and closer, and finally were almost upon them. The creatures seemed to be barking orders to each other, and dragging heavy burdens. Marcor felt a large depression in the cavern wall, pulled David after him, and they crouched into it. The creatures passed within inches, arguing and breathing hard.

The next time David and Marcor were not so fortunate. They had been traveling downwards for hours now. The voices this time were immediately near them, coming from another direction. Whether the creatures appeared from a different trunk of the caverns or not they could not tell in the blackness, but they had only enough time to squeeze up against the wall and try to let them pass.

David rammed his shoulders against the hard blackness behind him until he felt his bones would fuse into the roughness. He stopped breathing as they were passing by him, but one of their burdens rammed into his leg. The creatures stopped short and demanded vehemently in a strange language what was there. Almost immediately they were attacking David, and he felt himself thrown upon the hard cavern floor, with wet, rough hands reaching for him.

But suddenly, all motion stopped. The foul creatures were on the floor, and Marcor was thinking into David's brain that he had stunned them with his fingers applied to vital pressure points.

In the darkness, they could not ascertain what these creatures were, only that their body shape was humanoid, and that the burdens they carried were also humanoid. They had sacks with them which contained evil-smelling food. Without the black box, David and Marcor had no other source for sustenance, and already David's strength was at a very low ebb from lack of food. He ate of the evil-smelling flesh, trying very hard to keep it down.

As they continued to descend, the dangerous fissures in the cavern became more numerous and they had greater difficulty in edging around or leaping over them. They were now not very far above what lay below: black, solid areas surrounded by flowing streams of vari-colored liquids, some obviously molten metals and others looking more like water with steam rising from it. As David looked down at it all, he realized he could no longer keep the vile food in his stomach, and much more quickly than he had eaten it, he vomited it out. From then on, a fever began to drain more and more of his strength so that Marcor had to help him a great deal as they continued.

Perhaps they were getting careless; perhaps the entire floor was getting this way, but it happened as they were only a few feet from one of the largest crevices they had come across. They sensed no danger as they drew nearly to the edge of it, and before their instinctive reactions could jerk them back, they were falling through, taking chunks of floor with them.

David instinctively pulled his knees to his stomach. Marcor was holding him tightly as they plummeted downward, and before he knew it, they were plunged into the hot waters of one of the liquid flows. Down, down they went, hitting the hard bottom before the watery substance could fully cushion their fall. Marcor kept his right arm around David, and pushing upwards with his legs, they broke surface.

Vapors ascended all around them, and the liquid was unpleasantly hot. Yet it was far from boiling, and Marcor drove with his legs and free arm toward some black formations just above the surface, jutting out from the shore.

David was now almost completely incapacitated, able to aid Marcor only feebly in his struggles. When they finally reached the rocks, they lay there for nearly ten minutes, almost completely submerged in the liquid.

(173)

Marcor then struggled with him back into the current, letting it carry them downstream. David had neither will nor mind to protest, but could only struggle to keep his head in Marcor's hand, his face above the slimy wetness.

Each time as more shoals would appear along the shore, Marcor would swim over to them, and edge along them, peering through the vapors, searching for something.

Suddenly, as they came around a bend, two momentous scenes rushed into view. There was no more vapor—but only yards before them the liquid current plunged into nothingness. And on a great, shimmering plain to the right, atop perhaps a dozen rising rock tiers, rested Marcor's spacecraft!

Surrounding the craft, and all over the plain like colonies of ants, were hairy men, clothed in military uniforms of strange design. Staked out in various places were men spread-eagled face up, or bent into grotesque positions.

Marcor swam furiously to avoid the current's plunge, and reached the shore, dragging the earthling to the hot, dry rocks. It was perhaps five minutes that they crouched there unseen, watching the spacecraft and the thousands of hairy bipeds around it. Then, a scream burst out only a few dozen yards from their hiding place, and almost at once, hundreds of the creatures began shouting and running toward them, brandishing huge, wide-mouthed guns.

Marcor was instantly to his feet. He stood, eyes blazing, furious at the scene and burning with indignation. "Aelor!" he thundered. "Aelor-ké! Aelor-ké!" he roared again and again, starting to walk forward toward his craft.

In this dark sweltering of evil, the fierce, pure visage and his thunderings were so unknown and deadly to this place, like light to germs, that the foul creatures shrank back from him, as men blinded by the sun. It was almost physical pain as they shriveled before him in his fiery, righteous anger while declaring the name of his center of being.

David struggled to follow Marcor as they moved quickly toward the spacecraft, up the rock tiers, onto an ascending rung.

As soon as Marcor entered the craft, he leaped to the control panels and locked a force field which would freeze everything motionless but the craft itself for a distance of five light years. Then he rammed a lever all the way down, and the G forces flattened David aganst the craft's floor.

Even in hell, thou art there, David was thinking for the first time since he had found himself in this strange world. Marcor must have kept close to Aelor. He had known. Within just a few moments, there was a sudden shift and a terribly violent shaking. David slipped into unconsciousness.

* * *

When he awoke, Marcor was standing over him, smiling. The smell of his fever and the familiar clamminess were there; he was still weak. But otherwise he felt better.

David looked around the spacecraft. All seemed normal. It was after Marcor had fed him some thick vegetable liquid that he suddenly wondered. What *was* it all about?

He looked around him. He stared, fuzzy-cyed, at his surroundings. Now he wasn't even sure. Certainly he hadn't just dreamed *all that!*

Marcor was several minutes coming back, but when he appeared, David immediately asked him what had happened. Instead of verbalizing an answer, Marcor's face clouded, and he simply thought back some of the vividness of the experiences to him.

"But how could it be true?" David asked. "It was too bizarre, too nightmarish. Reincarnation absurdities . . . ."

Then he realized. If he had been feverish, dreaming it all, Marcor would have mentally followed the dreams and so would have experienced it all with him vicariously.

"Marcor, *tell* me. Was it a dream? A nightmare of all my own notions about hell? Or was it real?"

The bronze man looked at him for a long time, and finally said, simply, "I have observed many things I am not at all sure I would have wished to observe. I will only say this. If it was not a dream, it should have been."

·

14

It took David several days to recuperate from the fever. Therefore, he did not quickly notice the absence of heavenly bodies on the viewing screens as they sped toward earth. When he did notice and asked Marcor, the bronze man explained, "There are burnt cores and debris, but no living suns." He pointed to readings on a circular instrument. "Apparently these galaxies were consumed by a mammoth explosion. When you journeyed from earth, you went in a different direction and didn't see this."

Less than a day later, Marcor's conclusions about the explosion were substantiated, but with a stomach-wrenching twist. Identical with Earth's fixed position on their screen, a massive explosion was occurring. Everything up to that point was debris and ashes. David watched in chilled fascination. "It looks as if," Marcor surmised, "this chain reaction has been going on for thousands of years, destroying vast sections of your universe—and is just now reaching your home planet."

They steadily advanced to the brilliant radiations. Marcor unconcernedly adjusted his speed higher and higher. Then, as if the explosion were a blink in the night, they were through it, overshooting Earth by thousands of light years. Marcor arched his craft to reverse direction, and then took a new reading on Earth's predicament.

"Your planet is still there," he said finally. "We recorded the factors as we went through. The destruction is about four light years away from it."

They advanced closer and closer to David's home sun and planet, and before an hour had elapsed, David began to see continents which were familiar, yet strangely distorted from this perspective. They had whisked below the sun and were now orbiting over India. As David watched that nation's outline, like a stretched-out arrowhead lying in a bed of clouds, he thought of how easy it would be to land on any continent and find napalm and bombs, or famine and poverty, or prejudices and hatreds. And as he thought of it, his own land seemed not so much different. His mind rested on the Jerusalem Project. Surely if this cataclysmic an event were about to occur, the authentication of Jesus might be the answer to bringing the planet back out of the Evil One's grip before the end of planet Earth.

"How long before the destruction?" David asked. Marcor stared ahead, watching the continents, his fingertips on the dials. He did not answer.

It was mere minutes till they were, through Pélu's old coordinates, resting near David's house, concealed by a hill and some trees.

"Before you go," David said to Marcor, "there is one essential favor I *must* ask of you, one which your father promised me but could not fulfill."

Marcor looked at him, and nodded for him to go on.

"You must come to my home, and explain at least a little of this to my Charlotte. That is, if she is even there. She *must* know."

Marcor did not speak immediately. He seemed to be communicating as he stared off at the hills. Finally he said, "Yes. But not immediately. First I have one other thing to do for you. Then I will come."

With that they parted, and David stepped into the snow— yes, snow! He was surprised by it—and tracked his way through the inch or so of the white flakes to his front steps.

It was late afternoon and both of his cars were in the driveway. He knocked. No answer. Repeated knockings did not bring Charlotte to the door. Walking around the back and prying open a window, he gained entrance, then looked around his home.

It was much as he had left it, except that it seemed Charlotte was living here now. Food in the refrigerator. Clothes in the closet. Rumpled towels in the bathroom.

He took a shower, shaved, put on clean clothes, then sat around. But no one appeared. For minutes. For hours. Finally, as it got close to nine o'clock, he was hungry and decided to drive down to the shopping center for supper instead of messing up the kitchen. He left a note for Charlotte saying he'd be right back.

As soon as David wheeled into the shopping center, he saw that it was the Christmas season, with the usual decorations hanging everywhere and special sale signs enticing shoppers. He stepped out of his car into the wet sludge on the lot and, to avoid more, jumped onto the sidewalk. All around him heavily bundled bodies shuffled along, holding all sizes and shapes of bags and packages.

He stopped a moment, and looked up into the black winter sky tinged with the red and green shopping-center lights. The stars were bright, and as he stepped around the corner, he could see them clearly against the blackness. *Strange,* he thought. *All the stars I always thought were really there. But they're not. We're seeing only the light that left them dozens or hundreds or thousands of years ago. They're simply not there! As if it were a projection being screened in the planetarium, exclusively visual. Yet scientists and astronomers for years—or months—will keep calculating and exploring, totally unaware. But what should I do? Run around shouting there are no stars in that direction! The universe is exploding?*

He looked ruefully at the decorations silhouetted against the light-pricked night sky and wondered just how fast the explosion was occurring: the speed of light? Faster? Slower? When would it reach Earth?

Snow swirled around his shoes as he pushed open the jangling door of the hamburger shop. Christmas carols filled the shop as he joined the crowd of casual-dressed mothers and children, and the teens who dominated the place. A new off-beat version of "Jingle Bells" played, then "Home for the Holidays." Kids in line fingered designs on the fake snow sprayed on the windows.

A girl poured Cokes and handed the orders to the line of bundled bodies. David took his sack and drink and sat down at a small table.

The Coke was flat but the burger was good. He stared at the Christmas window scenes—a red-nosed reindeer and sleigh, a jolly Santa, a snowman, a pile of presents, a decorated tree.

He watched the people. Amazing how many were paunchy or skinny or bald—so few really attractive compared to people in magazines or on TV—or in Matter.

A fourteen-year-old boy surrounded by peers lighted a filter-tip and savored it knowingly. An exhausted mother with packages pleaded to no avail with her five-year-old to "Please stop stamping your feet—*please!*" Her older child sat quietly munching. Most of the snackers were talking, eating, hurrying. The garbage cans were too full . . . a malt was dripping from one.

A man sat down opposite him and extended his hand. "You're David Koehler, aren't you?"

"Yes." David knew his face registered surprise, and he resented the interruption. "How do you know my name?"

"I'm from *Life*. You mean you couldn't tell?" he asked, smiling good-naturedly. "This town is full of reporters looking for you!"

"What for?"

"You don't think the university kept your name secret, do you? They—"

"What *are* you talking about?" David interrupted.

The man smiled at him quizzically, and handed him the Christmas issue of *Life*. "The Actual Voice of Jesus Recorded!" it announced on the cover. "Scientists authenticate history."

David quickly fumbled his way to the inside story. With a Christmas slant, it took up twenty-two photo-filled pages and explained the findings in detail. So far, fifteen statements of Christ had been recorded. Each paralleled in substance the original translations' account.

"You'll want to pick up *Time,* too, and the others . . ."

David nearly exploded with enthusiasm. He talked at great length with the correspondent and asked repeatedly what effect the story was having on people. The answers he got on that were a bit vague.

"But this means Jesus *did* say these things! That the Gospels *are* accurate!"

"Well," the correspondent rejoined, "it's beginning to look that way. But much more work—"

"Oh, of course!" David interrupted. "But the *implications!* Jesus said He was *God*. He said He was the *only* way to heaven. He said He came from another world. His friends said that He rose from the dead. We thought it was myth!

Fantasy! Absurd! But if it's *really* true, do you realize . . . well, how can anyone dismiss it?"

The correspondent lighted a cigarette. "With difficulty."

"What about your own reactions?"

"How can anyone answer that fully? It's a great story. To our millions of readers, it's another unbelievable scientific breakthrough. And the religious aspects . . ."

The correspondent then deftly tried to move the conversation to facts about David, but the younger man was bewildered at the reporter's apathy.

In their discussion, they touched on quasars, antimatter, and the concept of an expanding universe, although David was careful to mention nothing about his trip or UFO's and insisted he did not develop the plans for the Jerusalem Project himself. He was so emotionally involved with all the experiences that he wanted very much to tell it all and talk and talk. But he knew he would sound like a lunatic.

After taking numerous candid shots of him, the man left. As David sat, staring after him, more people came, spread out burgers, shakes, Cokes, consumed them, shoved the remains into paper sacks, then left. More people repeated the cycle. None were talking about the fantastic Jerusalem Project

"Who was it—Shaw?—who said that Earth was probably an insane asylum used by all the other planets. Maybe there's a touch of truth to it," he mumbled to himself.

An old man in a very worn, wide-lapel jacket, baggy trousers, and cheap flannel shirt sat down by the reindeer and shakily pulled the paper from around his hamburger. His inadequate teeth made his chewing rather unpleasant. He was one of those who simply exist, David thought. What an absurd thing was old age—and this seventy-year-old shriveled before his time. How mystifying it would be to Paul, to Teca, this man already yielding himself mentally to be discarded like useless flotsam.

David spoke to him. They chatted for a time, and David finally shared the magazine article with him. The man's interest was superficial, and when David tactfully tried to suggest that as one approaches the latter years, he probably thinks a great deal of the next life, he seemed offended, as if David had brought up an unpleasantry.

David went back to sipping the ice water left from his Coke and looking at the magazines. The snowman decoration irritated him. So did the Santa. The tree. The red-nosed reindeer.

Finally, he turned to two high-school girls at the next booth, pointed to the article in his hand, and asked them if they'd read anything about it. They looked at him, interested. Both had heard about it on the radio, but they hadn't read the article. Apparently they assumed David was interested in something else, for they coyly invited him over.

Instead he took a walk. He simply wandered, observing the masses of people, all trudging through the slush on the melting sidewalks. They were there shopping because of a season which had the name of the All-Powerful who had invaded this speck of the cosmos to bring them the greatest victory possible. But that was just a slice of the motif—a reindeer, a snowman, and a star—yes, maybe in some places a star, and just possibly a cradle.

"Why *should* the Jerusalem Project work?" he suddenly demanded of himself. "They don't *want* Him. They don't *want* to know the truth. It's like Abraham said to the rich man— 'If an angel came back and told them, they wouldn't believe.' I fought Him the same way myself. If Jesus were walking around this shopping center, most would ignore him—unless he pulled off some miracles. It's just like two thousand years ago!"

When David arrived home, Charlotte had not yet returned. He waited for perhaps another half hour—till about midnight —and then he heard a car pull up. It waited in the driveway, engine idling, for some time. Then a man escorted a girl to the front door. A key turned in the latch, there was a short pause. Finally Charlotte entered the room, and the man returned to the car.

Almost immediately Charlotte saw the kitchen and den lights on and stepped back, startled. Then she saw David in the doorway, looking at her. Between the two of them, all the suspicions and anxieties flashed. Charlotte was alarmed at seeing him, almost shocked. David's mind was churning with unanswered questions about the person who had brought her home.

For at least a full minute they looked at each other. Then

(181)

David broke the charged silence by saying, "Charlotte, I'm sorry. Really I am. I had no way of getting back to you. No way at all. I'll tell you all about it and—"

"Don't," Charlotte stopped him, running to him and letting his arms move around her. "Don't for now."

They stood there holding each other for long moments. David put his hand under her chin and lifted her face to his. "I love you, you know," he whispered.

And the words he wasn't sure he would hear again came without hesitation, softly, sincerely. "I love you, too—very much. . . ."

15

David awoke as if he were emerging from a months-long dream. Stretching languorously on the queen-sized bed, he rolled over toward Charlotte, trying to put everything back together. A feeling of well-being was the dominant emotion he felt as he watched her eyes open and her arm reach toward him.

They had spoken of nothing last night beyond their hunger for each other during the time apart. They had expressed themselves in caresses and love, leaving all the other things unsaid.

Yet now they had to discuss them. David pushed the thoughts aside for the moment and kissed her. It was ten a.m. Saturday. They talked luxuriously about the weather outside, the joy of having each other close through the night. Then, breakfast. It was nearly 11:30 before they were through with their Swedish pancakes with lingonberry sauce, and coffee. David looked across the table at Charlotte and motioned for her to come and sit on his lap, as she used to do after their Saturday breakfasts. She did, her arms reaching out to encircle his neck.

"We've got lots to talk about." David began. "I've got a lot of explaining to do. But somebody'll be here—soon I hope—who will help me tell you. I'd be foolish to start without him."

He paused, and playfully tweaked her nose. "Now, maybe you can shed a little light on this Jerusalem Project and how the U. got involved. I see the equipment and plans are gone. Who'd you give them to?"

She explained about the Arco president and how she had run him out of the house with David's pistol, and then had immediately called the university and gotten several scientists over to the house.

David felt alarm for several reasons at this interest of Carlisle's. Yet he complimented his wife's audacity. "Nice work. Now you're in the heroine league. As little Shirley Temple used to say, 'I'm *very* self-reliant.' "

"Sure," Charlotte responded, with the same mock-dramatic tone. "Inspired by the artillery of my husband."

The phone rang again—it was the fourth time that morning. More reporters wanted to talk to David, but he brushed them off, saying to call back Monday. Charlotte smiled at him. "You think *this* is bad? You should have seen the way I've been hounded ever since the results of the project came back and the U. reported the source of the plans. And," she added proudly, "for an exclusive interview, I have been given a great deal of—" and she spelled out the next word slowly, "M-O-N-E-Y!"

David didn't know exactly how to respond to that, but it was obvious that Charlotte was not at all unhappy about the recognition and fringe benefits accorded her through David's UFO involvement. He asked her for copies of all the publications which had covered the story, and she answered that he'd have to get every current newspaper and magazine in the country. There was even to be a Christmas special on TV—obviously a natural for a network. "You'll be a celebrity, you know—even though I have no idea how you'll explain it all."

She was in such a good mood that David slipped in a comment about her arrival last night, "just wondering" who had brought her over.

Her face clouded, but she answered lightly, "Oh, I'd just spent the evening at mother's and Steve Forsyth offered to take me home. But *don't* think any silly thoughts, my love—he was simply an old friend offering a ride home."

David didn't pursue it, yet it troubled him and he determined there would be no more prolonged absences.

About 3:30 that afternoon Marcor appeared. He simply opened the front door and walked in without knocking; luckily David was the one who saw him first. He called out to Charlotte that they had a visitor, even before greeting his friend, then led Marcor into the living room where they could talk.

Charlotte's surprise at Marcor's appearance showed clearly on her face. But her curiosity soon overcame it. The university, the computer, the articles had all helped prepare her for this. She had a clear and analytical mind, and she not only listened to the story that David and Marcor related, but immediately began firing back questions. She was baffled and incredulous about the facts of the trip, Marcor's people, the spaceship, the different planets, the various modes of transportation, and extraterrestrial family life. It was too astounding to take in one gulp. Yet it soon became apparent that Charlotte had been reading a great deal about UFO's, and her references to various sightings, NICAP, recent *Look* magazine articles, and paperbacks on the subject all indicated her belief in "something more than the Air Force statements." Her excitement was very strong as she found herself getting answers to questions the article and book authors would have loved to have raised in that room. With the evidence of the Jerusalem Project's success, and Marcor himself thinking thoughts into her mind when words could not convey concepts, she found it hard to be skeptical of even the most fantastic aspects of David's adventure.

The fact was, it was nearly impossible for her to doubt even when the subject turned to Aelor and Jesus Christ. But her interest in this aspect of the story was vague, for somehow it didn't seem relevant. Yet she listened.

"If," David said, "we could just tear off the dull-image, 'religion-is-a-bore' skin that encases our thoughts about Him, we'd realize how exciting He is. We'd rush to him, like I'd go after steak! But until you've tasted it for yourself, it's like trying to explain what fresh tomatoes taste like to someone who's never even seen one. . ."

(184)

Marcor thought to her, "Aelor in you is life itself, like the flow of life through a tree, or the song through a bird, or light splashing a planet."

"But you must ask for him to flow through you, Charlotte, as I did," her husband explained. "You must say you want to be on his side, obeying his orders."

They talked like this to her at great length. Charlotte, her mind reeling, listened and watched them, and eventually agreed that they must be right.

"Give Him all that you are," David implored, looking at her with great emotion. "Ask him to let the Aelor-force flow through you, and control you."

She nodded, her eyes dropping from his, then closing. David bowed his head to pray and asked her to repeat after him in her mind.

"Did you ask Him as I said?" David whispered when she lifted her eyes.

Again her head nodded assent, and David went to her, hugged her, a rich joy of fulfillment and release from an ominous gray shadow in his heart.

Before long they were talking again of spacecrafts and planets as Marcor answered more of Charlotte's questions, and David attempted to fill in. But he realized it would take months to get it all across.

By late evening they had hardly let up in their excited talk, only grabbing a snack for dinner. David had not known such joy in all his life . . . he felt at one not only with the universe, but with the one who was part of him.

It was about eleven o'clock when they were interrupted by a knock on the door. David answered it, and he found Carlisle and two of his men standing on the front steps.

Anger surged through David as he thought of this man's actions toward Charlotte. He was about to say a few brief, cutting words and slam the door in his face when the executive said, "We've come to talk to you about Phelps. You *were* the last to see him alive, weren't you?"

It was the first time that Phelps had entered David's mind since his return, and his emotions instantly turned to concern. What tie did Carlisle have with Phelps' coming out here that last day?

He invited the three men in. When Carlisle saw Marcor sitting beside Charlotte, his eyes narrowed, but he said nothing. He simply sat on the couch as he was bidden, and started probing about the last time David had been with Phelps.

"Nothing!" Carlisle explained. "Absolutely no trace of the man, and we have every reason to believe he was with you. As was Jamieson, who rode with Phelps, and whose body was found in *Vermont!*"

"What 'every reason'?" David asked, fully alarmed.

"Don't get clever . . . you may hear the answers in court," Carlisle warned. "You both disappeared about the same time . . . not long after the Clint Edwards session, if you'll recall. Now, who is *this?*" he asked, looking at Marcor.

The bronze man was dressed in clothes patterned after David's, and except for his skin, height, and features, did not seem totally out of place. Marcor stared back at them and then asked a strange question. "Who is this Clint Edwards?"

The men looked at him strangely, and Marcor followed with, "When will that happen?"

Shortly after this, abruptly, all three of the visitors rose, moved to get their coats, and without another word walked out the front door.

Marcor was still sitting there when David came back from the door. The man from matter looked at his earthling friend and explained, "There was much of the Twisted One in the minds of those men. I could sense it as they talked to you. And when he mentioned the man Edwards, there was something terrible in their consciousness. When I asked the questions, the answers were quite clear."

"What?" David asked.

"Edwards is to be killed in Boston the night of January 28. It will be accomplished by none of these men, nor even by anyone they know. But it will be when he is on television."

David did not know how to react. The thought was absurd, and all he could think of to say was, "But Clint Edwards is their employee."

"They have strange thoughts in their heads of using this to their own gain," Marcor explained. "That is why I sent them away—with no memory of tonight—for they were no good here."

(186)

They talked about the situation for only a short time, agreeing that Edwards had to be warned. But Marcor insisted that he have no role in it. He had to return to his own people—and would not come back to Earth.

The goodbye which followed was far more emotional on David's part then he had anticipated. Up to this point his feelings about Charlotte and getting home had left no room for thoughts of his leaving Marcor and what a change that would make. But now as he was saying farewell to his last link with these extraordinary things, he felt a great sense of deep loss.

"But," Marcor remonstrated, reading his mind, "I am *not* your last link with the extraordinary. You are just as linked to it now as ever—if you continue to choose to be."

With that he parted, with not so much as a hint of sorrow, only stating that they would surely meet again in the joys before them.

*   *   *

The next morning after breakfast, David took a short walk alone by a nearby stream which was covered with snow-misted ice. The thoughts of his still being linked to the powers of Aelor filled him with a deep sense of well-being. He spun around to survey the sparkly world around him. What joy to be relaxed, to be attuned to the One who had made it all. He exulted in the colors, the ice, the black branches etched against the blue sky, even the new, metallic-gold Pontiac parked in a neighbor's drive. He exulted because Aelor wanted him to like colors, to like things, to rejoice with Him in His creation. David whipped himself around, ran, kicking up snow in delight, leaping over the creek in the ecstasy of unity with creation, with Aelor.

The thoughts of what lay beyond this creek and sparkly snow—the hatreds and diseases foisted by the Twisted One and man's own bent nature—lingered in his mind. That was the smell of death, like cancer through lymph glands. But right now it was the *cure* of this death that made David alive. What fulfillment in joining forces with Aelor to war against the Twisted One by missions of love, of caring for people!

He watched a little girl, all bundled up, out in the yard playing with her daddy, who was helping her make a snowman. Nostalgia for his own childhood seeped into him. How terribly brief a human's stay on earth! How hard when one gets old enough to realize that the years are rushing by! How hard to accept a changing body, a decaying body crumbling toward other worlds. How quickly the girl would grow, the man would age.

That afternoon David purposely turned to the book of Ezekiel, remembering its implications from his previous readings. He started at the beginning, and carefully thought about each chapter. About halfway through, he laid it down, awed by not only this writing, but his own experiences. Was he to be compared to Ezekiel, who had been transported to such fantastic worlds? With Earth now near its climax, would others have experiences like David's, the way Isaiah and Jeremiah had in Ezekiel's time?

But David shuddered at the thought. It seemed sacrilege. He was no author of Holy Writ!

Yet, as he contemplated, it seemed that Aelor was forcing into his mind: "Every Christian breathing, with the Spirit of Myself pouring through him and out into the world, is part of the fullness of the Aelor-force."

That afternoon he also leafed through Isaiah to look at portions he had previously underlined. One verse—51:6—hit him with new impact. "Look high in the skies and watch the earth beneath, for the skies shall disappear like smoke, the earth shall wear out like a garment, and the people of the earth shall die like flies. But my salvation. . ."

Aelor's salvation. It was being ignored! And here the smoke was only four light years away, whatever its rate of approach. Certainly there would soon be "signs" in the heavens: stars blinking out! What would people's attitudes be *then?*

He shared these thoughts with Charlotte. Neither Marcor nor David had previously mentioned the explosion approaching, and when he told her that afternoon, for the first time since Marcor's appearance, a shade of disbelief crossed her face. She did not say David had made it up, but it was apparent that even if she thought it were true, she did not particularly *want* to believe that . . . nor, in fact, to talk so extensively about all these biblical implications David kept bringing up.

The week that followed was a kaleidoscope of activity. David chose the magazine to which he wanted to grant interviews, and signed the exclusives for $15,000 beyond what had already been paid Charlotte.

Since the Arco corporation gave him an icy reception when he called about his old job, he accepted a position as a PR man with the university. Before making that decision he had spent extensive time with the professors who were directing the Jerusalem Project. He looked forward to being near their further developments, and they were delighted with his involvement and strong interest.

He tried hard to contact Clint Edwards. But he learned—not only from run-arounds when he made phone calls but also through the mass media—that Edwards had indeed become a very big property of the Arco corporation, storming nation after nation and building a vociferous, animated following throughout the world. He seemed to press all the magic buttons. Since he was impossible to contact, and David's name was not exactly magic at the Arco corporation, he took his problem to Carla Adams. Sitting at dinner with both him and Charlotte and delighted at their togetherness, she agreed to get him a ticket to the company's New Year's party for executives and "friends." It was to be in New York; Clint would be present.

*   *   *

The train gave one last jerk, then was still, and the jam-packed car began emptying itself. David walked through the old high-roofed New York terminal and the double set of doors to the icy breeze outside.

A few blocks away, the entrance to the amphitheater was carpeted with bobbing swarms of people. Most were wedging their way to a window marked "Redeem Sears Coupons for Tickets." His was a Sears coupon, so he began maneuvering for shoulder space to shove toward that counter.

The closer he got, the more solid became the mass of bodies. Most were young girls in colorful winter coats. They wedged tighter and tighter, until David could literally have lifted his feet from the pavement and been suspended there. After some fifteen minutes of twisting and angling his way in through the solid walls of imitation leopard furs, black car coats, and thick sweaters, he got his ticket and began the fight out of the center.

After he was free, David straightened his coat and tried to look as mature as possible as he walked through the turnstiles and up to the balcony. In the seat next to David's was a paunchy, amiable young man.

"Jeff Wilson?" Carla had twisted a PR assistant's arm to meet David here.

"Sure 'nuff," the young man replied, extending his hand.

"Nice of you to meet me."

"Would have been sitting here anyway."

David sat down and looked at the sections of people in the audience below, squared off like so many fields of circus-colored wheat, little heads bobbing and swaying, barely discernable as individuals. Eventually a long-haired foursome walked to center stage to scattered screams of recognition. David tried to hear the singers' voices but they were largely indiscernible above the audience response and the Big Sound they competed with.

He stared out at the euphoric, pulsating sea of young energy, responding with every bit of bounce in their bodies to something they could identify with, something theirs. They were made to *respond*, to get caught up in a vast, rollicking thing bigger than themselves . . . and David couldn't help thinking of the magnificient diversity of music he had heard beyond the quasars. *If these kids could but hear it!*

"Crazy," Jeff Wilson was whispering. "Look at 'em." A slight grin touched his mouth. "They think with their glands."

"Not all of them. There's some great social criticism in the contemporary musical idiom—if they can just see it in perspective."

Clint strode confidently out to center mike. Screams and applause drowned out his voice. The beat shook the auditorium and he moved his lips and body to the angry sounds of "The Relics." The kids throughout the audience responded, mouthing the words. Jeff Wilson whispered throughout the performance about Edwards' concepts and fantastic abilities. He seemed to have made a personal idol of the singer.

After the performance, David tried to get backstage to see

Clint alone and talk to him before the party. But neither Jeff Wilson nor the young blue-jacketed guards were in the least bit helpful. So he and Wilson headed for the party, and decided to walk since Arco was only six blocks away, and this was such a crisp, pleasant night.

The streets were black except for occasional street lights and murky yellow rays from behind bolted store fronts. A block and a half from Arco, three eleven-year-olds on an unlighted porch started taunting them as they passed. Handfuls of pebbles came flying and struck both of them on the back.

Wilson turned quickly and glared at them. The boys stood, leering but ready to run—or scream. Finally the young PR man walked away cautiously, keeping his angry gaze on them.

"Damn niggers!" he spat as they approached their destination. "Just 'cause my skin's white! Bad as Southern racists."

David looked over at him. "Didn't think I'd hear you use that term."

"Nigger?" Jeff asked, "No, I don't for Negroes. For people who are willing to get their hands dirty with us whites and make something of themselves. But then there are niggers—blacks who don't give a damn!"

"There are whites like that, too," David pointed out.

"Sure! Sure there are."

There was silence for a short time as they walked. Then David said, "The situation's monstrously complex."

"*Of course!*" Wilson retorted immediately as they entered the Arco building. "What's needed is *laws* and *communication*. Show whites the Negro tragedy. Show Negroes somebody cares."

"Do we?" David asked sharply. "Do I care about those boys out there? Do I care for people hurt and poisoned by environment and twisted values as much as I do people hurt by disease or accidents? Do I love even KKK members, while hating their actions and demanding justice? Bitterness—it's the same as between Indians and Pakistanis, Arabs and Jews, Ibos and Hausas. Communication, laws—we need more. But it's got to be love for *everybody!*"

Jeff smiled. "Sure. I've heard plenty of songs about that. But there are still stinkers who have to be *forced* to give justice."

"True. *Very* true. But if we despise any people—racists

(191)

black or white—we become the same as they are. We must go to the one Source that—"

The elevator they were on suddenly opened and they were interrupted by a large crowd of people chattering in the hallway. After they had wedged their way into the line for *hors d'oeuvres,* Carlisle came walking up to them with a slender wine glass in hand and a very beautiful young girl in arm.

"Here's our enigma now," he said, waving his glass delicately but dramatically.

David smiled uneasily and held out his hand. Carlisle, on shaking it, asked with a confidential smile, "Be honest now, Koehler. Don't you think that *Life* reporter went a bit overboard with all those innuendoes about your 'mystique' and 'spiritual depth'?"

"Absolutely," David agreed, taken off guard. "Just one conversation over a hamburger. I couldn't have been that mystical."

"Well, I'm glad you were able to come to our little family get-together. Too bad you're *not* one of the family. But as long as you have friends . . . like Phelps . . . By the way, whatever did happen to him?"

Carlisle peered steadily into the other's eyes, and although David blanched a bit and felt his fingers become icy, wishing Marcor had erased more of Carlisle's memory, he returned the gaze and said, "You wouldn't believe me if I told you."

The older man kept staring intently. Wilson nervously interrupted with, "You probably wouldn't quite believe his hippie ideas either, like just love *everybody*—the Klansmen who hangs you, the mugger who knifes you—just *everybody.*"

"Did the flying saucers tell you that?" Carlisle abruptly demanded of David, his piercing eyes and malevolent smile lighting his face.

David started, and paused a moment. "No—as a matter of fact," he said at last, "a man from outer space did."

"Oh?" Carlisle's eyes lighted just a fraction more and the others looked at David, wondering if this were merely a word game or if he were really serious. "What did he say?" Carlisle probed.

"That we're all doomed."

The girl with Carlisle gave a nervous laugh, as if she weren't

(192)

quite catching on to the joke but should be laughing just then. "Doomed to be blown to bits?" she asked, smiling coyly.

"Something like that. But we have a chance. If we accept all this Man tells us and obey him, we won't be destroyed."

"And what does he tell us to do?" the girl asked.

"Get to know him. Open our wills to him."

She shuddered. "But what does he plan to do to us? If he controls our wills, he could make us do *anything*."

"Precisely," David rejoined. "He'd enable us to live without fear or prejudice. If we gave our wills to his power, we'd discipline ourselves, use sex the way it was intended, treat our bodies—"

A voice from the side floated in sharply: "Sounds terribly restrictive." It came from a well-known Big Sound artist who walked up, clothed in brilliant red, green, and black, a petite blonde snuggled up beside him. "Bound to lead to unhappiness," he added, grinning and looking down at the girl.

"The opposite, I assure you," David declared.

Wilson cut in with introductions, then explained, "Koehler here is taunting us with a riddle."

"Sounded like a moralist for a moment there," the singer commented. " 'The Relics,' so to speak," he added, glancing at Clint Edwards, who had just joined them.

Carlisle started them all moving toward the ballroom where most of the other guests had already assembled. But he never took his gaze from David's eyes. "Tell me," he asked, "who was this space man's reception committee? Were you there?"

David returned his gaze. "No. Not too long after his arrival, He was murdered."

"Well," the girl smiled in mock relief. "If he's dead, we're not doomed after all."

"Oh, I didn't say He was dead. Just that he was murdered. And earthlings are certainly doomed if they're without him."

Clint was growing impatient. "Come on—who are you talking about?" he demanded.

"I refer to the Man who made your body. And mine. The Man who formed the entire earth and every molecule. His name is Jesus Christ."

The reactions were mixed. Clint laughed good-naturedly but with obvious discomfort. Wilson and the girls followed suit.

(193)

The singer punctuated the uneasy laughter with, "Ah, a Bible-thumper in the midst!"

"Well, you've read about David's experiments," Carlisle explained. "Scientific restoration of words, and finding the authentic sayings of Jesus. Interesting hobby." Carlisle was again staring into David's eyes, even as the conversation swept on. He didn't divert them until a man slipped up and whispered a message, whereupon the magnate unobtrusively slipped over to the nearest window, opened it a crack and stared down. Others moved over to him, and in a moment they heard the ugly sounds from below.

"Well, the race riot's here," Carlisle remarked casually.

Ten stories below, mobs of dark figures were rushing through the streets. Glass crashed. The faint sound of a woman's scream hung in the distance. Something like gun shots echoed far away between the stubby steel canyons.

Carlisle quickly closed the window. "Wish I had a dozen grenades!" he said, his teeth working against each other. "Drop 'em out the window and blow their black guts to Triborough Bridge."

They quietly moved away from the window, but within ten minutes half the guests had caught on and were apprehensively crowding against the glass. More windows were opened, and a cacophony of violence swelled from the streets below. They closed them and began to talk out their fear, realizing what could happen, little groups chattering self-consciously about trivia or discussing the figures down there and the scant police forces. Fear mounted stronger and stronger, for shouts could now be heard about burning the buildings. The fears built hatreds. Clint's comment—"If they get ugly, machine-gun them!"—was not unique. The singer opened a window, took aim at a crowd of black forms far below, and pitched the liquor bottle in a high, arching dive at them.

"Clint," David asked, watching the faces of the people in the room, "tell me something. Who *did* kill Maria?"

The husky athlete was startled by the apparently irrelevant question. He didn't bother to answer.

Soon, the first thick black billows of smoke boiled skyward past the windows.

Panic was almost instantaneous; everyone was caught in a

mad rush for the elevators. Both were jammed full far ahead of David and Clint. Screaming, desperate men and women fought against those inside the elevators, who were shoving and kicking the newcomers away from the doors so they could shut them.

David hit Clint on the shoulder and motioned toward the stairs. They pried and squeezed themselves loose, darted to the swinging door, then ran, half falling and sliding on the guard rail, smelling the smoke getting denser each floor they descended, trying to blink it out of their eyes. Dozens of others were close behind them.

Suddenly, about six flights down, the stairs stopped at a swinging door through which he and Clint crashed into a service and kitchen area. The air here was searing hot and smoke obscured everything beyond ten feet except for hungry little tongues of red flame dancing in the haze.

They found the stairway on the other side of the building, but heat and flames were roaring below and it obviously led to the inferno. David stumbled back toward the swinging door, searched all along the kitchen, and after at least two long, long minutes found a window with a fire escape! He screamed for Clint to join him.

He screamed again, hesitated a moment, then scrambled back into the kitchen yelling Clint's name. He was fully across to the other side of the building when he saw him, moving blindly away from a high wall which was aflame and trembling.

Fear multiplied the sting in David's eyes and the pressure in his chest as he stumbled toward that quivering wall which was poised to flatten them both. A horrifying thought rushed into his mind: *Was this a well-planned trap by the Twisted One to kill me? Surely that Evil One doesn't want me alive!*

He was at Clint now, and pulled him toward the doorway. The two of them stumbled forward as the wall shivered, and with a slow, ponderous whoosh, it crashed in at them with a heavy crunch which smashed through the fire-weakened floor, leaving a huge hole behind them.

They made it to David's window, and though the metal burned their hands, they scrambled out onto the fire escape and half slid, half ran down the heated skeleton to the drop-off below. Once they had their feet on the sidewalk, they ran desperately to clear the area and did not stop until they stood among yelling Negro onlookers, watching the flaming building from a block away.

They stood there only a few seconds. "The fall of the house of Arco," David reflected softly, the dirty-gray building now a gaudy display of flames, crowded fire escapes, and screams. Rocks were being hurled at the blackened faces of firemen running out hoses and directing vehicles. A handful of police were trying to face down the crowd. On the top floor windows of Arco, tiny puppet figures waved arms eerily in the smoky, red-tinged air. Sideways, like a crab, one figure moved out, then plummeted earthward.

Clint was pulling David away, and he readily followed toward what seemed to be empty streets. They walked swiftly, alertly, wanting to run, or dash into a dark building for safety. But the unfamiliar buildings threatened to spew out rioters.

"Whitey!" The Negro's ominous scream tore into David's stomach and throat, but he didn't turn his eyes. He kept pace beside Clint. Then, from the side, he saw a group of black figures running—but not in their direction. He and Clint turned the next corner and walked hurriedly.

They had fled only a few blocks from the fire when David noticed a Negro boy about eight, lying on the ground against a warped post of a decrepit porch. He stopped and knelt by the boy. Brown eyes stared up at him. He was blackened by soot and smelled of smoke and fire as much as David. A blood spot stained his upper arm. His jaw and cheek were gouged, as if he had run full tilt into protruding, rough bricks. Open flesh and oozing blood accentuated the distorted shape of the jaw.

"Come on, Koehler!" Clint demanded, grabbing David by the arm. "Let's move!"

David was pulling his handkerchief from his pocket as Clint used stronger and stronger expletives to get him up from his knees. "Wait just a *second!*" David objected. "Nobody is helping the kid in this frenzy!"

But before David could say more the athlete had turned and was striding rapidly away. David's calls had no effect on him.

Although he had little idea what he could do for the child, David at least stopped some of the bleeding and used a piece of his shirt for a direct pressure bandage for the arm. The boy was still conscious, staring at him through his wall of pain.

"You'll be okay, boy," David said to him. "Just relax and we'll—"

At that instant the boy, having slowly lowered his butchered jaw and parted his lips, spat impassively into David's face from deep in his throat.

David wiped it off with his blue silk handkerchief and looked down at the white spittle mixed with splotches of red. He remained kneeling there for long seconds, then said, "Guess if I were you, maybe I'd do the same thing . . . maybe."

It was less than a minute later that David was aware of people around him. He gently laid the boy down and rose, turning to the group. About six Negro men stood in a semicircle around him, staring.

"We've got to get him to a hospital," David explained. "He must have been in that fire."

The others stood silent.

No one moved. The six men looked as if they were enjoying the face-off.

"We've got to get him to a hospital," David repeated.

Another lengthy silence. Then, a thin, wiry one with glasses said, "Yes, you're right. We do."

At that moment all six men moved forward and were quickly upon him, swinging the butts of .45 automatics. David dropped to his knees, then rolled back and attempted to flip himself up but was caught by a cutting blow right above the eyes. He brought his knees up to shove out at them but then was smothered in a sea of hot, oppressing weight. Then came another hard blow on the back of the head.

16

David typed savagely with two fingers, letting his emotions carry him from line to line:

The tall, white-haired man stood with his brother—the two of them against thousands ready to kill them. He had invited them there for a showdown.

The lone leader stared out at the angry mob, then gave a command for everyone to step away from the ringleaders.

No one moved. Most averted their eyes, looking at the ground. But slowly, under the fierce gaze of the white-haired man before them, they separated. Soon the ringleaders were alone confronting that awful gaze.

"If these men die an ordinary death," he thundered, "God has not sent me. But if God makes a new thing, and the earth swallows them up, you'll know these men have provoked Him!"

The ground began shaking. Suddenly the ringleaders fell screaming into the maw of an earthquake's awful cleavage. Then fire roared out and killed 250 men who had sided with them.

David pulled the paper from the typewriter and started revising it. He exulted in creating something. If only he could somehow communicate what really had happened in the Bible —how this Moses represented more adventure than a dozen Westerns, facing down the mobs again and again and walking right into a thundering mountain. Moses' life changed history because of the power beyond himself. Moses was linked to it just as David knew he now was. No one was fully alive without this reality and power!

He walked across the room and sat in his easy chair. How could he communicate all this? Even Charlotte didn't really seem to understand.

To add to his concerns along the same line, he had to approach her on his wanting to give away large chunks of their money. He was afraid she wouldn't see the need of it and he felt strongly apprehensive about even bringing it up. In fact, he was beginning to feel that way about bringing up any of his feelings that they should give more and more of their lives to Aelor.

Charlotte's voice interrupted his thinking. "What's the bear working on now?" He looked up to see her head poking around the corner, the same old impish look of happy intrusion on him. "Something to spread abroad the good name of the U. and its most prestigious project?"

"I hope so." He handed the sheet of yellow manuscript paper to her. She read it through, then wrinkled her nose.

"I don't get it."

"The man is Moses," David explained. "I'm trying to show how the awesome force of the Creator has been active in lives which changed our world—and how the Jerusalem Project is at the center of it all."

Charlotte sat down on the arm of the chair and handed the paper back to him. "But don't you think you're getting away from the promotion the school wants you to do? Weren't some of the administrators rather dubious about your trying to apply everything in the project to modern life—and to them as well! I mean, David, let's face it, if you push too hard and too fast you're going to lose their respect—and also, if not your job, certainly your chances for promotion."

"Is that my only goal?" David responded, a bit perturbed at her. He stared at his wife, then reached for a magazine and leafed through some pages until he came to an article on modern Israel which he had marked extensively. "Modern life?" he asked. "The Jerusalem Project not applicable to modern life? Listen to this sentence on the first page: 'Arabs and Israelis together could make the Middle East a garden. But there is no peace; the Middle East is a mess.' Now, Charlotte, you can't tell me that we don't need to apply the Jerusalem Project! We need more than the musty scholar-approach to antiquity that just writes up reports and publishes them only in unread journals, with an occasional writeup in *Time* and *Look*. I tell you, it drives me out of my gourd to see all these fantastic, world-changing facts under everybody's nose, yet mostly ignored except for publishing books and articles about it! When I try to draw implications on how to apply some of these words we're researching, I get the educator's stare, as if it's irrelevant to the stated purposes of the study. Nuts! It's *relative* to our every breath, our every emotion. It was certainly relative in New York a few weeks back with rifles and jeeps and thirty buildings destroyed and deaths—yes, 342 dead and 2,063 hurt *that they know about,* and me in the hospital a week —just because we've been ignoring *precisely* this."

Charlotte was nodding her head and saying, "You're right, David. You're right. Just don't be a bull in a china closet! Get across your concepts, but don't alarm people by going at it the wrong way. And don't ruin your own future by antagonizing people unnecessarily."

David looked at her without speaking. Finally he asked, "*My* concepts, Charlotte? Are they just *my* concepts?"

"Of course not!" she replied quickly. "They're what's true. I know that. I just mean—"

"Charlotte, this may be the wrong time to bring this up. In fact I *know* it's the wrong time, but I'm sure there'd never be a better time, so I might as well do it now." He paused. "I doubt I'll be able to communicate what I feel in this, so try—really try with me—to understand."

She smiled uneasily, and David abruptly said, "No. Forget it. Let's talk about it later. Right now, let's talk about Clint Edwards' show tonight, let's celebrate something. Let's—"

"No," Charlotte insisted. "Let's talk about whatever *you* wanted to talk about. You act as if I've got the mind of an ogre."

David took a long, deep breath, and settled deep into the chair. Then he took her hand and squeezed it affectionately. "Charlotte, you know I don't think anything even close to that. It's just that I have a feeling that hit me, and maybe you won't see it the same as I do, that's all."

He got up, replaced the magazine in the rack, then stood looking across at her. "You've heard about the story of Jesus and the widow's mite—how Jesus watched rich people contributing money and then this old, poor woman who dropped just a couple pennies into the box. Jesus said to his disciples that she had given more than all the rest of them combined *because she gave all she had.* She didn't just skim a little off the top. She gave till it *cost* her something.

"Now, Charlotte, we just give a few dollars to United Fund and all that, yet look at all the people who are miserably poor, who are in need in hundreds of ways. How can we make all these plans for a plush home in suburbia and the car and the clothes and the whole works with all this money? How can we use it so there will be no struggle at all when so many around us are struggling to keep any sort of self-respect, and struggling without really knowing what life's about?

"I tell you, Charlotte, it hit me very, very hard when I thought of all I have and how little so many others have, and me not giving a *thing,* really. And as I thought it through, I couldn't help but think that the least we can do is rake off 20 percent. We can simply rework the whole budget. We have so much now. There no reason why we can't."

Charlotte did not respond for quite some time. No expression crossed her face, and when she finally did say something, it was not at all clear to him what she was thinking. "It may be that you're right, David. We'll have to do a great deal of thinking."

Watching his wife, he suddenly wanted more than anything else to pour his thoughts directly into her brain, as Pélu or Marcor could have done, to make her feel as he did. But she wasn't affected. She wasn't driven to want to give of herself, to want to spend this time walking and communing with the One who gave love. Charlotte was happy to see David sacrificing for a job that would build prestige and finances, but she was increasingly impatient with the time he spent walking with Aelor or searching through his Book. Yet she had *said* she believed! He could sense no oneness with her about this focal point for his life, but how could he rectify it?

They began talking about little things, but the irritation remained. "We're just cranky because the show is tonight," Charlotte said, interrupting David's wandering thoughts. "Clint comes on at nine, and both of us can hardly stand the tension, and you know it!"

It was true. "Maybe I really don't want to watch," David said. "I'm not at all sure I do."

They looked at each other, frustrated because there was nothing more they could do. "They *have* to check your letter out," Charlotte said. "Even if they do think it's from a crank.

You composed it so well that the only thing that really looks crazy is implicating Carlisle. But if the FBI looks into something like that, it's bound to be covered properly."

"I keep thinking and thinking," David answered. "But there's nothing more to do. Clint hasn't listened to me, no matter how much I force myself upon him. The trouble is, how do you stop a rifleman with a scope!"

"*TV Guide* says it will be the most-watched special this year," Charlotte commented. "A thing *that* big, surely they'll have safeguards. Of course, if Carlisle really did set the thing up . . . he'd have the insider's precision. But maybe the whole idea was just a put-on somehow. Maybe Marcor just saw some dumb TV plot in their minds."

They talked on and on about it. When the time came after supper for the hour-long special to begin, they were so psyched up that their stomachs were tight.

It came on with brilliant color and fast-change motion. It was one of those magnificent productions with lavish theme sets, arty photography, and lively choreography. The decidedly unique factor was that this show did not simply skip from song to song and from thought to thought. It was cohesive throughout the entire hour. The show mounted in intensity: from black-and-white sequences of sets depicting poverty and the anguish of "Maria"; to a tree with a dangling noose by a soft-green riverbank with a shanty in the background, for "The Evening's Entertainment"; to a rushing, wildly colorful dance sequence expressive of modern vitality as opposed to "The Relics." At the very beginning a commercial introduced the show, but after that nothing broke the viewer involvement which steadily increased with the visual and musical impact.

It was live, with Edwards on stage at Boston's largest and newest arena. But many of the sequences had been filmed before so that both the Boston audience and the millions watching by TV saw on a half dozen different screens a fast-moving, powerful display of color, sound, motion. Edwards would be singing live, orchestra behind him, and then the scene would blend with creative cinematography and shift to a wide-screen film sequence of him on a different set.

As David and Charlotte watched the production unfold, they were caught up in the strange power of this anger against injustice, anger against those who allowed the riots and anguish and poverty. They were so wrapped up emotionally that even though they knew Carlisle might have planned a murder, they were caught almost as off-guard as the rest of the nation at the unbelievable thing which happened just as Edwards finished his last song.

A gigantic explosion ripped the scene on the stage, and in an instant the screen blacked out. There was nothing at all visible for several minutes, until the screen finally focused on a shocked commentator staring into the camera, shuffling papers and saying something had happened, but they had no reports as yet and were awaiting word from Boston. Within the minute he was handed a news bulletin which he quickly scanned, then began to read. He told of an explosion which apparently had killed Clint Edwards and several others. Fifteen minutes later, it was confirmed, and a planted bomb blamed as the death weapon.

After the first half hour, reports started coming in about riots: not racial, but youth attacks against symbols of the Establishment such as city hall, municipal buildings, police stations.

And now, David thought as he watched, *they'll say it was a conspiracy because of my letter and blame the Establishment directly. Of course, maybe they'll get Carlisle and see the plot. But what plot? I still don't understand it all one bit. What can I do now? Tell Clint's body, "I told you so"?*

The next weeks were ones of mixed emotions. David felt apprehensive about Arco, Carlisle, and possible repercussions from the Phelps incident. He wanted to know what everything represented and why in the world all this was happening in the pattern it was. He despaired at the increasing violence which followed Clint's death. Whether that vaporous hell David had spent time in had been dream-thoughts or real, he knew that these patterns would have made up a very acceptable "bag" there.

At the same time, he was forging stronger and stronger his link with the preternatural by his own patterns of communication with Aelor. He struggled to draw a frame of reference on the basic problems at least, and one verse especially seemed to hold a basic answer for him: "The world's sin is unbelief in Me."

It was from the Gospel of John, and it was from this same book that David hit upon a concept which revolutionized his thinking about how he should live his life in the little time remaining. In the 14th chapter he kept coming upon phrases like, "If you love me, obey me." "The one who obeys me is the one who loves Me." "Anyone who doesn't obey me doesn't love Me." He saw this tie-in closely with the next chapter, especially the following portions:

"Take care to live in Me, and let Me live in you. For a branch can't produce fruit when severed from the vine! Nor can you be fruitful apart from Me.

"Yes, I am the Vine; you are the branches. Whoever lives in Me and I in him shall produce a large crop of fruit. For apart from Me you can't do a thing.

"If anyone separates from Me, he is thrown away like a useless branch, withers, and is gathered into a pile with all the others and burned. But if you stay in me and obey my commands, you may ask any request you like and it will be granted!

"My true disciples produce bountiful harvests. This brings great glory to My Father. I have loved you even as the Father has loved Me. Live within My love.

"When you obey me you are living in My love, just as I obey My Father and live in His love.

"I have told you this so that you will be filled with My joy. Yes, your cup of joy will overflow!

"I demand that you love each other as much as I love you."

IMPOSSIBLE! How could anyone obey a demand like that? How could David love other followers of Aelor as much as Aelor himself did? David knew he simply did not have it! What fantastic love Jesus Christ must have toward his Father. Could David Koehler love that much? Absurd! Yet this was what Jesus was demanding. What was David to do? Browbeat himself? No hypodermic could inject this love into him. And if it were not in him already, how could Jesus expect him to create it?

This line of thinking brought up other statements by Jesus that he realized had frustrated him before. Commands like

"Love your enemies." That *sounded* marvelous. But how could he really *do* it? If Carlisle were to come here and give Charlotte a hard time, or accuse David of murdering Phelps and Jamieson, would he feel love toward him? Impossible!

And then there was that totally undoable command of Jesus': "Be ye perfect, even as I am perfect."

How *could* he!

Yet Jesus was demanding it of his disciples, of anyone who followed him, not as an option but as a demand, if David were reading at all correctly. How could this be?

It took a great deal of walking, pondering, and praying that God would give him insight before he came up with meaningful answers. But when he did, the concepts revolutionized his approach to living.

Yes, the commands *were* impossible. That was why Jesus had come—so that the Aelor force so alien to this planet could flow into the lives and emotions of beings who thirsted after it. David couldn't love as Jesus had. But if he asked his Creator to love through him, that was possible!

But how? It couldn't be that cut and dried, that easy. What was the way he put this into practice? What were the specifics he could *act* on?

Here is where the verses about obeying fit. David knew that every time he would take time to get alone, to communicate heavenward, he was able to get direction on what he should or should not be doing. Deep within, he more and more consistently sensed what actions, one by one, Aelor desired. But often David knew he did *not* obey. He did not always refuse more calories when he should have. He did not always break away from an entertainment to spend time with Aelor when he had already put it off. He did not always speak out about his link to his Creator when the right time was there. In many decisions each day, David knew he could obey, or he could slough off what he knew he should do.

And the call was to *perfection*. Obedience to *every* call.

That was frustrating! The only way it made sense to him was to think of a football coach who demanded perfection. Each player had to strive to be perfect on *every* play, straining *every* muscle, using *every* mental ability. He might do something wrong, but if he were *striving* for perfection and content with nothing less, he was digging toward victory. But if he set his sights lower, he might as well quit: he'd never taste the sweet joy of triumph.

David spent a great deal of time studying the life patterns of Jesus, and again and again these concepts were fortified. More and more David saw that his involvement during the time left on Planet Earth—his money, his energies, everything —must all fit into the basic patterns Jesus lived.

But it was precisely this emphasis—and his time spent in pondering these things—that was driving a wedge between him and Charlotte. It was not that she complained he was wasting his time. And he was very careful to spend hours with her, both working around the house and taking her places. It was just that his minutes with God always seemed to come at the wrong times. In reflecting on the situation, he realized that no matter when he scheduled his time with his Creator, it would interrupt *something*.

The conflict grew inexorably more pronounced. Yet David was continuing in his philosophy of reaching out for perfection and tasting the delights of running his own body and emotions instead of letting his body and emotions run him. He saw, too, a good thing in Sunday. Jesus had said that the Sabbath was made for man's benefit. To David it seemed like the ideal opportunity to spend some chunks of time with Him. But when he broached the subject with Charlotte, she tersely suggested, "Why not just build yourself a vault in the basement and meditate down there? You'd be no more dead to me than you are now. What am *I* supposed to do all the time? With me going to school and you meditating all the time, how can we do *anything?*"

Charlotte was exaggerating, wanting to lash out at something because she didn't share his new interests.

"That's not fair," David answered. "Whatever needs doing, I'll get it done. And you know there's still *plenty* of time for being together and going places and the whole bit. We've done lots of things together. Only—"

"Only you're going a bit overboard, aren't you? You're simply *not* living like a normal person!"

David stood abruptly and stared for a long time into her eyes. Finally he said, tersely, "I hope not!"

It was after this episode that the cleavage regarding money, time, and activities became more and more pronounced. It seemed incredible to David the way Charlotte was resisting what she said she believed in. Yet the more David thought of it, the more he realized how incredible Pilate's denial was, when he knew Jesus was innocent. How incredible the Rich Young Ruler who backed away from Jesus because of what it would cost, though he knew Jesus represented truth. How incredible all the people accepting the facts of the Jerusalem Project but doing nothing about it in their own lives. Yet David himself had fought it like a tiger. Why not Charlotte? Apparently, though it had appeared she'd opened herself to Him, she had tasted nothing at all of the dynamic Aelor-force.

The thing that worried him even more was that he had learned from Charlotte's own mother that when Charlotte visited with her, Steve Forsyth would often happen to be there at the same time. David did not know whether to confront Charlotte with this. But as the weeks passed and their relationship grew increasingly strained, he realized he had to. Unfortunately, he first mentioned it one Saturday at breakfast, as they were arguing about the funds he wanted to give to Project Self-Start in their community, and the personal time he thought they both should devote to it. Piqued at her attitude, he blurted out that he knew she had been seeing Steve Forsyth.

Her face flushed and her eyes blazed. Then she looked down, pursing her lips. "Who told you?" she asked quietly.

He looked away from her, a pained expression on his face. Finally he said, "That's immaterial. And I don't want to make a big deal out of this, Charlotte. But let's get at the root of this thing. You know as well as I do that the friction between us is that Someone else is now more important to me than you. But, Charlotte, if he becomes more important to *both* of us, then he can draw us together instead of splitting us apart. We can join to serve him and know a joy better than anything we've ever tasted!"

She nodded, as if tired of hearing the same speech again and again. The thought of Steve filled her with ambivalence. Old feelings of affection were growing. The mystique was there. She felt that Steve was more like her now than was

(207)

David. She had serious doubts that she had married the right man. Of course, Steve Forsyth was quite certain she hadn't, and was very persuasive when with Charlotte.

"Guess I just don't have it," she muttered, her eyes looking down. David tried to lift her face with his hand, but she pulled away, still looking down at the table. "How do you know," she asked, "that He wants each of us to live the same way?"

David thought on that, leaned down and kissed her cheek. Was he heavy-handed, trying to press her into his own mold? "Maybe you're right," he said. "I'm sorry. Really I am."

There was a lengthy silence. Then, "We'll make it different," she whispered back. "We'll make it different."

But in the days that followed there were more disagreements and more angry words. David's efforts to control himself were not always successful. One day after one of their breakfast spats he had to cover a story for the university and didn't return home until seven o'clock that night. When he pulled into the drive, he noticed the Renault was gone. And inside, there was no one waiting with dinner, but there was a note on the table.

Charlotte had left, and this time she had taken all her belongings with her.

17

David looked at the colorful Pan Am calendar on his wall. Three days before Easter.

What did it all mean? How could Charlotte have betrayed him? How had he even been involved in the Arco affair—the murders, the violence, Carlisle?

Arco. He feared it.

All these external weights hung heavily on him, and within

there was little to counter them. He had never felt so empty, so dry. Even when he tried to communicate with Aelor, he felt he was simply talking to himself. The warm, joyous emotion of God within was strangely absent. He felt discouraged, a failure for not laying hold on God somehow and getting back the old impact and force. Something seemed to block him from spending enough time with God to "break through."

He also knew fear. What would *Arco* do to him?

He walked into his den. In each room, objects reminded him of Charlotte, and of things they had done together. He stared at the easy chair in which they had sat, chatting on and on while eating one of her special snacks. A late snow was whirling against the windows. He remembered the time she had been so excited about the biggest snowfall of the season when it was heaped high, almost to the window. She had dared him to go out with her and romp in it. But he hadn't felt like it, so she had barged outside alone and run around to this very window, hip deep in snow and covered with the wet stuff, tapping on his window and grinning like a white-splattered pixie.

Every room reminded him of talks, of touches, of pictures they had bought together, drapes they had chosen, records they had given each other.

They had loved each other. They *had!* Yet David's involvement with the "Prince of Peace" had ruptured their love. They were totally different people now. At least *he* was.

But this couldn't be! Jesus was supposed to bring peace and love!

David remembered that Jesus had told his followers he had come not to bring peace but a sword, and that because of him families would break up—that Jesus would divide husband from wife, father from son. But David found that too terrible to accept. It had proven true in his own life, but surely that wasn't what Christianity was supposed to do—break up marriages! And Charlotte had believed in Jesus! She had said those words. Were they nothing at *all* more than lips in motion?

He sat there in the den, and looked again at the letter she had sent him a week ago, a letter which spoke nothing of their former joy but only of their finding themselves now and their planning for what would be best for each . . . and that Steve Forsyth *did* enter into her thinking about the future. That's all she said about him, and David wasn't sure he would have wanted to hear more.

A strong desire—almost like a hunger which was life-and-death insistent—began working in him. If he could but drop this whole thing, live a "normal" life, and give his whole energies to making Charlotte and himself happy as he had before, he could win her back. He knew he could! After all, she was still his wife. He could!

He watched the stars outside, and even in the midst of these thoughts he wondered how many of earth's telora were out there somewhere, watching him like a huge grandstand section viewing the drama below, act by act. He wanted to grasp the reins of his life, go to Charlotte and do whatever necessary to bring her love back to this house.

The stars were cold, icy diamonds above, impervious judges watching the mortal wrestle below. The thoughts could flow through his mind, the desire could work strongly on his emotions, but he knew he could not turn his back on that which was basic to his living, no matter how dry he felt at the moment, no matter how desirous of feeling Charlotte close to him and holding him and whispering her love as before.

After long moments of looking at those distant suns above, he sank slowly to his knees and yielded himself to the power and plan of Aelor-ké, whatever that plan might be, however obscure his part. He did not feel heroic in doing this. He knew he had no real choice, if he were not to destroy himself.

As he knelt, he once again prayed for Charlotte. He repeated in a whisper some memorized words of Jesus from John's Gospel:

"In solemn truth I tell you, anyone believing in Me shall do the same miracles I have done, and greater ones, because I am going to be with the Father. You can ask for anything, using my name, and I will do it, for this will bring praise to the Father because of what I, the Son, will do for you. Yes, ask anything, using my name, and I will do it!"

Though David believed in the promise, at the same time he did not really feel that anything would happen to change Charlotte.

Wasn't there something about *his* having to have the faith in order to have his prayer answered? He felt faithless, empty as a discarded water skin. Yet he kept praying, in desperation, having no other recourse. He knew he could not communicate the reality to Charlotte . . . he had tried so often. And now he did not even feel the reality within himself.

* * *

The air breathed the crisp life of spring as Charlotte and her mother walked between the thick, rectangular pillars at the cemetery gate. Each Easter morning they had come, year after year, to visit the family grave site.

Occasional unmelted patches of the winter's last snow were scattered across the dried grass. They walked over the three little hills which lay between them and the markers. Unless a stranger were to read the sign at the entrance or look closely at the slight rises in the grass which indicated the flat markers, he would not think it a cemetery but a pleasant park, with thick evergreens, high maples, and great expanses of lawn.

A bit of snow covered that special marker as they got to it. Charlotte knelt and gently, reverently brushed it off with her gloved hand. The plate had her father's name and two dates: birth and death. Just beyond were two half-size markers, each with the name Barbara inscribed, with two dates on each. To the right of her father's marker was an identical plate with her mother's name. It bore only the birth date.

To see that always chilled Charlotte. And it chilled her even more to know that the ground beneath her feet was, in her mother's mind, reserved for Charlotte herself. No plate was there—but the ground was.

As her mother stood at the marker, Charlotte's eyes wandered. A few yards away fresh earth was peaked by a spray of large yellow roses, shriveled, ugly, with snow gently whipping against the brown edges. On the far hill, a tall man and a wee girl dressed in bright stripes walked slowly away from a grave. Charlotte stared at them for a long time, until they disappeared into the valley.

She left that special place and wandered a few yards away, reading other names and dates, reflecting. There was a much wider variety of ages than she would have guessed. On a fairly new brass marker she read the name "Mary." The date on the simple plate of brass was only two months after Charlotte's birth date. Yet this Mary had been laid to rest here just about two years ago.

Charlotte picked off one of the black peels of bark from a dogwood tree, then plucked a blossom and moved the stem slowly between her fingers, appreciating the reddish, pinched edges on the sturdy bloom.

Her mother was still standing at the grave. Charlotte looked up at the cemetery's single monument looming to her right: a massive, simple cross, two giant timbers of rough redwood poking into the sky.

She went to it, her feet crunching the little gravel walkway, and finally stood gazing up at the warm, wide-grained wood. On a metal plaque at the base was an inscription of the Lord's Prayer. She ran her fingers over the raised metal lettering, then read it slowly:

> Our Father, which art in heaven
> Hallowed be thy name
> Thy kingdom come, thy will be done
> On earth as it is in heaven.
> Give us this day, our daily bread,
> And forgive us our debts, as we forgive our debtors.
> And lead us not into temptation, but deliver us from evil
> For thine is the kingdom, and the power, and the glory forever.
> Amen.

Charlotte put her fingers on the rough wood of the cross and leaned her shoulder against it, still toying with the dogwood blossom in her hand.

She saw her mother coming toward her. Deliberately, she pushed her weight away from the wood and walked toward her, rolling the dogwood petals between her fingers, then absent-mindedly dropping the bruised flowers on the white gravel.

*   *   *

It took a great deal of courage for David to pick up the

phone and dial. He hated putting himself in such a vulnerable position, but he was determined to try anything possible.

Charlotte's mother answered, and it took several minutes for her daughter to come to the phone.

"Hello?"

"It's me," David said. "Hope I didn't get you up from a nap or anything."

"Just reading."

"Look, Charlotte, we're not enemies or anything. . . ."

"Of course not, David."

"Charlotte," and here he stammered a bit, "I'd like very, very much to see you. Just *see* you. And talk to you a little. Why couldn't we have a date? No gimmicks, no sob stories. Just to see each other."

There was silence for a long while, and David had to ask if she were still there before she responded.

"I guess so," she said. "I'd want to be back early."

"It's a promise. How about coming here for dinner Saturday at six?"

She hesitated again, but finally agreed.

All Saturday afternoon, David straightened up, cleaned, and generally made like a housewife. He set the table as Charlotte used to, and put her favorite records on the stereo. Still empty inside, still despairing of a reconciliation, he nevertheless prayed for one. And prayed. And prayed.

Her knock startled him even though he was expecting it. Glancing at the settings on the table, he walked to the door and let her in. The smiles and greetings were strained. He took her bright yellow coat, then seated her at the table in their small dining area.

"This will be quite a switch," she said, trying to be light and humorous. "Will you wear an apron when you serve?"

"Definitely not," he answered with mock indignation, walking into the kitchen, then reappearing with the peas and potatoes. "One more trip and it's all ready."

He reappeared with two thick steaks, placed them on the table, then sat opposite her. The thought crossed his mind that he could say, *I would have lighted some of those tall, white candles we like so well, but then you might think I was trying to get romantic,* but he immediately realized, *No, no that won't do!* It seemed that everything he might say would be taken wrong, or seem defensive, or have something to do with the Jerusalem Project or Aelor, or his wanting her back so much that even now he couldn't stand the absurdity of their eating at this table together, with the same pictures around them, the same dishes, the same records easing music into the room yet their being strangers soon-to-part.

David said a brief grace, then handed her the steak. "Sure you don't want to try some A-1 sauce this time?" he offered.

She smiled. "I refuse to change the delicious taste—if the smell is any indication." They were able to continue such table talk for a time with the passing of salt, peas, potatoes, coffee, and the buttering, stirring, and pouring of it all.

"That painting is just beautiful . . . I've always liked it so much," Charlotte said, staring at the pastoral scene of a creek and meadows.

"Mmmhmm," David agreed. "Draws you to it as if it's real." Again, he felt crosswise. Should he tell her that since she liked it so well she could take it with her? But add "while you're gone" to indicate he wanted it to be temporary? Or not bring it up at all?

"How are your classes coming?" he finally asked. "Almost graduation . . . just a few more classes, then finals, huh?"

"Lot of busy work," Charlotte replied, putting her fork into her baked potato. "Only interesting classes I have are psych and English lit. That's 'cause of the profs. The rest is just a mountain of paperwork to go through and get tested on."

Why was it when she talked about her classes and graduation that the feelings in David's chest built up toward tears starting in his eyes? She would be graduated soon and he would not be a part of it, maybe not even invited. He didn't even feel free to ask her where she would be working or living after that or what her plans were, for it all came right back to their relationship. They talked on for about twenty minutes, a bit on trivia, a bit on current events and music they liked. David guarded his words, steering clear of their estrangement and his involvements and thinking. As they talked, he felt far more depressed than he thought he could possibly be with Charlotte right across from him.

(214)

"How is your work coming at the U.?" Charlotte asked.

"Fine. Sometimes I wish I could be directly involved with the Jerusalem Project instead of just writing about it and the curriculum changes and the president's travels. But it's interesting."

"What do you think of the possibilities for advancement? Or do you think you'll go somewhere else before too long?"

"I don't know. I really don't. It depends. I just want to do whatever . . . Aelor commands." Her expression didn't shift, so he went on with hesitation. "There must be *something* of significance I can do on this twisted, miserable planet. Whenever I watch the violence on the news and read of the napalm and Africans killing Africans and Pakistanis and Indians killing one another and the whole bit . . . I want to *do* something about this wretched world. But I'm just not in a position to."

Charlotte's face was now showing signs of agitation, and David stopped talking.

"Don't, David," she asked quietly. "Please don't talk like that tonight."

She did not say it unkindly. In fact, it seemed almost like a little-girl plea. But it gathered all the factors into a combination of emotions too strong to be bottled up in David's body. He slowly, heavily let his face sink down into his hands, acutely aware of Charlotte's presence yet at the same time unable to stop his open expression of emptiness and despair.

"God, how can you *do* this to me? Why did you ruin us? You said *anything*. You know what I'm asking . . . why can't it be!"

He sat there, his face buried in his hands, weeping, hating the spectacle he was making of himself.

Finally he lifted his head, and tried to look at Charlotte. But, as he blinked the tears from his eyes, he realized she was not sitting across from him any more. Panicked, he ran to the front door, but as he passed the living room he saw her sitting on the couch. He walked slowly to her, watching her sobbing, her slender fingers digging into the pillow and her face buried in it.

He stood there silently, watching her, waiting as she wept and talked into the pillow. Hope was flickering in David's chest, but he could not presume.

When she sat slowly upright and began to dab at her eyes, David went to her and looked into her face.

A new light—and love—was shining from her eyes.

Late that evening they stood together outside near the creek. A corn-yellow moon, which did not seem very far away at all, floated above. David grabbed her and swung her around, in the joy of mutual understanding and oneness. She had tasted it! She had felt, somehow, the electricity of Aelor!

Yet, in all his joy, on the edge of his mind was the thought of Arco. Of the wars. The killings.

Arco was an enigma. What had it all been about? He could fathom so little. How did the murder fit in? The riots? The wars? Communism? The coming destruction? What ultimate role did each play? He felt as if he held a tiny flashlight which stabbed but a tiny thin beam into miles of foreboding blackness.

For all the horribly destructive forces on this twisted planet, however, life was bearable. In fact, joyous.

David had raised someone from the dead! He had brought dynamic into a dead human, lightning sparking into the Planet of the Shadow of Death.

He had been dreaming of global, heroic exploits. But this new thing was the miracle. He, one human with Aelor-life, could reach out and be the means to let life flow into another. He hadn't done it himself, but he had been the tool used.

"Life!" David shouted as he lifted her playfully by the elbows.

She bounced back to the ground, sharing his exuberance, and laughing with him. "I never understood it. Not at all," she said. "It's *real*. It's not just words or emotions. I guess I sensed all along the reality of what you had. But I felt empty inside myself—and I couldn't give in. Something drove me from it."

"Life," he said again. "Charlotte, wherever we are, whether we feel close to Him like this or dry as Death Valley, we *can raise people from the dead! He* will *through* us! Maybe we can't always stop the napalm or make the world a garden of love. But, the way Adam brought physical life to this planet just one at a time, so can we. So can *anyone* with Aelor-life!"

She looked full into his face, then up at the moon above.

(216)

"What can I say?" she asked him. "Before, when Marcor was here, I was just repeating your words. Orthodoxy according to St. David. But now, it's a total . . . well, I can't express it . . . like tasting something delicious that compares with nothing else 'cause it's unique. I didn't want to be controlled by Someone else. I even considered giving you up so I wouldn't. But being involved with Him and—now I can see why you really *want* to!"

David hugged her with one arm as they began to walk along the creek. "We can ask *anything*. That's what He said. I could have asked more for Clint. I wish I had. *Anything*. He's ready to act! Even to help us on all the little problems we'll face—like finances and scheduling our time with him and—" he smiled—"our own little nasty tempers!

"And you!" he added, looking down at her, then rubbing his nose on hers. "Yes, you, my lovely flesh-and-blood Charlotte, *you* God raised from the dead!

"Here is a miracle.

"We can reproduce *life* on this desolate planet!"

About the author:

HAROLD L. MYRA, publisher of *Christianity Today* and president of Christianity Today, Inc., has given solid editorial and biblical leadership to the magazines published under the auspices of that organization: *Leadership Journal, Leadership 100,* and *Campus Life,* as well as *Christianity Today.* Dr. Myra was formerly editor and later publisher of *Campus Life* and vice president of the publishing division of Youth for Christ International. He has written more than a dozen books and contributed significantly to the editorial design and format of *Reach Out* and *The Way,* best-selling editions of *The Living Bible.*

Dr. Myra holds a bachelor of science degree in education from East Stroudsburg State College in Pennsylvania and was awarded an honorary doctorate from John Wesley College in 1977. He and his wife, Jeanette, have three children: Michelle Leigh, Todd Stephen, and Gregory David.